Copyright © 2001 by David E. Twichell

All rights reserved. No part of this book shall be reproduced or transmitted in any form or by any means, electronic, mechanical, magnetic, photographic including photocopying, recording or by any information storage and retrieval system, without prior written permission of the publisher. No patent liability is assumed with respect to the use of the information contained herein. Although every precaution has been taken in the preparation of this book, the publisher and author assume no responsibility for errors or omissions. Neither is any liability assumed for damages resulting from the use of the information contained herein.

ISBN 0-7414-0

Published by:

INFINITY
PUBLISHING.COM

Infinity Publishing.com
519 West Lancaster Avenue
Haverford, PA 19041-1413
Info@buybooksontheweb.com
www.buybooksontheweb.com
Toll-free (877) BUY BOOK
Local Phone (610) 520-2500
Fax (610) 519-0261

Printed in the United States of America

Printed on Recycled Paper

Published January-2001

The UFO - Jesus Connection.

By
David E. Twichell

For:
Laura

Table of Contents

Acknowledgments
Preface
Part One: UFOs AND THE PHYSICAL REALM
Chapter 1 1
Chapter 2 7
Chapter 3 15
Chapter 4 25
Chapter 5 33
Part two: JESUS OF NAZARETH AND THE SPIRITUAL
Chapter 6 41
Chapter 7 49
Chapter 8 57
Chapter 9 65
Chapter 10 73
Chapter 11 85
Part three: THE CONNECTION
Chapter 12 97
Chapter 13 109
Chapter 14 121
Chapter 15 129
Conclusion 141
Author's note 149
Figures 1 through 8 151
Bibliography 157
Articles and Other Sources 159

Acknowledgment

I would like to thank Giorgio A. Tsoukalos of The Legendary Times for his assistance in research for this book. He, in close association with Eric Von Daniken, have brought startling facts to bare that are reflected herein. (http://www.legendarytimes.com)

I would like to thank Barrie M. Schwortz (photographer for the Shroud of Turin Research Project.) His web site (http://shroud.com/index.htm) not only provided a wellspring of information, but he personally reviewed my work to make certain that the scientific evidence presented was accurate.

I would like to thank my wife, Laura. Her assistance in research proved invaluable, and her moral support was the reason this project went forward.

Preface

The ancient astronaut and Biblical UFO hypotheses are not new. However, no one seems to want to take the matter to the next logical step. If Ezekiel's "wheel within a wheel" and Moses' "pillar of fire and cloud" were forerunners of today's UFOs, then the Star of Bethlehem and the brilliant cloud to which Jesus ascended must be treated in the same vein.

How can one make a connection between ufology and Christianity without suggesting that God is nothing more than an alien in a flying saucer? The two concepts appear to be so far apart that an expansive void exists between them. The answer is to bridge that void with knowledge.

Although I have presented many documented cases in this book to dramatize the immense volume of evidence supporting the existence of the UFO/abduction phenomenon, I have not necessarily written it for the expressed purpose of convincing the reader of its reality. I present it to dramatize the evidence that led me to the conclusions of my own belief system.

Too many people feel that their belief system is the right one and are close minded to any theories based on the facts. Even though their own beliefs are based on "faith" that flies in the face of all known facts. Their parents, grandparents, priests, ministers and rabbis have formed their reality. It is much easier to let someone else do their thinking for them than to analyze the facts for themselves and draw their own conclusions.

This fact is why the "Flat Earth Society" still exists to this day.

"The Bible says that angels guard the four corners of the Earth. How could the Earth have four corners if it is round?"

"If the Earth was round, when Jesus comes back down from heaven, He would slide right off. How could he light on a round Earth?"

This is the kind of logic that has been passed down from generation to generation. It is much more convenient and less thought provoking to accept this logic than to use one's own. Copernicus was imprisoned by the church for such heresy as suggesting that the Earth is not the center of the universe. Some people hold this concept to be true today.

When I was in grade school, before the first space flight, my science teacher told us that if we were to go into space, we would find that the Earth was green. This color was a reflection of the earth's foliage off the ionosphere. We learned that the Milky Way was one of only seven galaxies in the universe.

Mainstream science thought they knew everything there was to know at that time, as they do today. Now we look back one hundred years and laugh at their arrogance. At the turn of the twentieth century they looked back one hundred years and laughed at *their* arrogance. I have a distinct feeling that at the turn of the twenty-second century, they will look back at the science of today and laugh at ours.

If the truth runs contrary to the conventional world view, so be it. Mainstream science, throughout history, has consistently proven that the truth runs contrary to the world view of the previous century.

And what of an afterlife? A heaven . . . or a spiritual realm? Communication between souls, living and dead?

Fifty years ago ESP (extrasensory perception) was so much nonsense. A parlor trick. Today it is not only accepted by mainstream science, it is used to explain away virtually every unknown phenomenon of the mind from spirit communication to the near death experience. Too many incidents have occurred in my life to dismiss out of hand the existence of this phenomenon.

If we, as a race, are to evolve technologically, emotionally and spiritually, we must be willing to accept the facts that we learn along the way and not dwell on the dogmas of our ancestors. Not that what our ancestors witnessed and reported were incorrect. Much to the contrary. Perhaps it is a simple matter of interpretation. Over the centuries we have learned that the clash of thunder and the streak of lightning did not indicate that the gods were angry. We have learned that the moon was not something to fear and throw stones at. That the eclipse of the Sun does not mean that it is being devoured by a dragon.

The proper knowledge yields the proper interpretation of any phenomenon. Does this mean that to accept UFOs as a reality we must throw out all we know and believe about the Bible? Should we listen to those who say, "you can't believe in UFOs and God too."? Once again, much to the contrary. The trick comes with integrating the new facts with the old. Scientific and intellectual development is much like a good mystery novel. The facts are laid out for all to see, page by page. If one is able to recall the clues given in chapter one and incorporate them with the ones given in chapter ten, it won't take a Sherlock Holmes to figure out that the butler did it before the final page is turned.

The volumes of clues, that the world has been given, at the time of this writing, are enormous. If we keep the clues given in the Bible separate from those of science, we must have two different belief systems. If we weigh the mass of evidence gathered from around the world, concerning UFO and spiritual phenomena, against that of mainstream science, then two other belief systems are born. There are virtually as many belief systems in this world as there are believers. Yet, I can assure you, there is but one reality. If that reality is a culmination of many dimensions, then that is the *one* reality to which I refer.

I have spent the last thirty-six years studying the UFO phenomenon . . . pro and con. I have studied metaphysics . . . pro and con. I have studied mainstream science and the Bible. For every question answered, there are ten more questions posed. If I were to subscribe to one paradigm as gospel, I would have no choice but to throw out all other known facts in spite of the legitimacy of their existence. It is by finding and incorporating that common thread that helps to make the puzzle complete.

What I propose in this volume may not be the last word on the matter. It may well be as far off base as one could get. However, it is a theory based upon the culmination of my findings and personal experiences through the years. I ask you only to examine the evidence, add your own knowledge and personal experiences and draw your own conclusions. If you are right, you're right. If not . . . keep digging.

Do not think that to even consider such a hypothesis is blasphemous. Blasphemy requires the element of intent. If one *intends* to degrade, discredit, or otherwise distort the truth regarding something held sacred, this is blasphemy. I can assure you that such is not the intent in this case. To examine the evidence and arrive at an erroneous conclusion is simply a mistake. I cannot imagine a loving Father who would banish his own child to an eternity of torment for seeking the truth and drawing the wrong conclusion.

Now open your mind. Let's explore!

David E. Twichell

What are these ships that skim along like clouds - like doves returning home? They are ships coming from distant lands, bringing God's people home. They bring with them silver and gold to honor the name of the Lord, the holy God of Israel who has made all nations honor his people.
Isaiah 60: 8, 9

You cover yourself with light. You have spread out the heavens like a tent and built your home on the waters above.
You use the clouds as your chariot and ride on the wings of the wind.
Psalms 104: 2, 3

PART ONE

UFOs AND THE PHYSICAL REALM

Chapter 1

In the summer of 1962, I was fourteen years old. The average fourteen-year-old, who wasn't above pulling a prank on anyone if I thought I could get away with it. Harmless pranks of the "Ha-ha, I made you look," variety. My parents and sister were the most accessible, thus the most frequent victims. It naturally follows that they were the first to grow weary and begin approaching my claims with caution.

At about 11:00 P.M. one Saturday evening, I was off to bed. My bedroom light was off and the window was open. I caught something out of the corner of my eye and did a double-take. The sky was green! Not completely green. A large patch of billowing smoke with seemingly bright green lights behind it was in the sky about 200 feet above the ground.

"Mom, the sky is green," I announced in a stunned tone.

"Go to bed," my father said patiently.

"No, really, the sky is green!" This time with more emphasis.

My mother strolled in and looked out the window. *My God, I hope she sees what I see, or I'm a nut case!* "Earl, the sky is green!" She called to my father in amazement. *Thank you, God!*

My father and sister jumped out of bed in unison and ran to the windows on the side of the house where we were. "What is it?" Mom asked of my father.

"How should I know," was his retort, as he threw on his robe and headed for the front door. The rest of us were close behind.

The four of us gathered on the front lawn of our westside Detroit home and stared into the night sky. It was dead quiet. Even the incessant chirping of the grasshoppers was absent. Fifteen minutes earlier the only thing in the sky was a mass of stars. Not so much as a cloud. Now there was a mass of billowing smoke. By this time it was directly above our house. It was no longer green but multicolored. The thick smoke was illuminated from the other side by huge electric lights. As the smoke began to clear above our heads, we could see giant round flood lights of

1

yellow, red and white. I don't recall most of what was said between us but I do remember us commenting about the lack of any sound.

My sister, three years my senior, huddled against my mother, who tried to console her and herself at the same time. I, the fourteen-year-old adventurous macho man (and not too bright), was more amazed than frightened.

"Look!" My mother called. Off to our right, a pillar of smoke was descending slowly to the ground. It was as if a jet of air was forcing it down. "It's the second coming!" My mother declared.

I was not quite ready to go to my glory after fourteen short years on this planet but if it really was the "second coming" I knew there was no hiding from Jesus. "Let's run to Him!" I heard myself shouting.

"You stay right here!" My mother ordered.

Thank you, God! I stayed put.

We looked back up over our heads to find that the lights had receded. The smoke was so thick that it made an outline of this silent craft impossible to discern. Yet the huge round colored lights still shown through. As bright as those lights were, they never illuminated the ground where we stood directly below.

We continued to watch in silence as the smoke slowly dissipated, leaving only the cloudless, star-punctured sky.

We returned to the safety of our house, unscathed. I do not remember talking at length with my family about the amazing "smoke and light show" we had just witnessed but it was over now and there was church to attend in the morning. We went to bed.

The following morning my father bought the Sunday morning Detroit Free Press to see if there was anything on this strange event. Sure enough, others had seen it. Some had reported it. We had not. The authorities wasted no time in handing us an explanation. They were the northern lights! With all the confusing technical jargon they could muster, a weak case was made for the northern lights making it all the way down to southern Michigan.

"Those weren't the northern lights," I argued. "I've seen them in pictures and in movies. Northern lights are ribbons of different colored lights that streak across the sky. And they don't have smoke with them either!"

"Well," my mother assured me, "if they say they were the

northern lights, then that's what we must have seen."

It might be understandable that a fourteen-year-old boy from Detroit couldn't tell the northern lights from a sack of onions. My mother, however, was born and raised in northern Michigan. My father had spent two years in Alaska. They had seen the northern lights on more than one occasion. Yet my father had stared into the night sky in awe and apprehension. My mother was all set for the Judgment Day!

It was at that very instant that I realized that we were being lied to. Not *us* in particular. Not anyone who had witnessed the event and knew the difference. They were lying to those who did not see it. Whom would those people believe? Us or the United States Government? The experts on the matter. The ones who are sworn to serve and protect. The ones who are paid with our tax dollars to tell us the truth about everything - especially what goes on in our air space.

And so the matter was dropped. At least as far as my family was concerned. I have not dropped the matter to this day. Nor will I!

At that point in time, I was not aware of the frequent UFO sightings around the world. The now famous "Roswell incident" had occurred the year before my birth in 1947. It had long since been dismissed by the general public as a case of mistaken identity.

The United States Air Force personnel of the 509th bomber wing in Roswell, New Mexico, from the general on down, had mistaken a weather balloon for a crashed flying disc. This is the bomber squadron that housed our nuclear war heads. "Fat Man" and "Little Boy" were dispatched from this facility. The debris field was three quarters of a mile long. The Air Force quarantined the entire area. They drove out truckloads full of debris. They made an official announcement to the press that a flying saucer had crashed. Then the next day they said, "Whoops, we made a mistake." They held an emergency press conference in a small office at the base. The remains of a shattered weather balloon were strewn across the floor for the world to see that all was well. The naysayer could go back to saying "Nay" and the rest of us could sleep well.

At any rate, I was totally unaware of the phenomenon. Later in life, after I found out the frequency of worldwide sightings and how the Air Force would scramble fighters to intercept them, I recalled another incident when I was about ten years old. It was 1957 or 1958. The fire station, which was located about three quarters of a mile from our home in Detroit, would sound the air raid siren on the first Saturday of each month at 12:00 P.M. We were used to this test and thought nothing of it. One Wednesday afternoon about 3:00 P.M. the siren began to wail. My father was at work. My mother, sister and I were in the house when it started and my mother immediately became concerned. I don't know if my sister understood the implication of the situation but I didn't. All I knew was, if Mom gets concerned, I get concerned. The three of us stood at the dining room window, looking skyward. About five minutes into the ordeal, two Air Force fighter planes, dispatched from nearby Selfridge Air Force Base, zipped over the house.

"If I tell you kids to go downstairs, don't ask any questions - just go!" My mother ordered.

We stood and watched a while longer but there were no explosions - just the incessant wail of the air raid siren. After a few minutes the siren sounded "All clear."

The next day the papers informed us that someone had accidentally hit the switch and turned on the siren. I thought nothing of it at the time but, after considering what I had learned in the following years about the Air Force's approach to the UFO problem in conjunction with this incident, the red flag in my head went up.

Not withstanding human error, why would the Air Force scramble fighters unless something unknown had been picked up on radar?

The Air Force, at the beginning of the modern UFO era, would scramble fighters to intercept the intruders. In some cases they would fire on them. More than once the flying discs almost started World War III. America thought they were Russian. The Russians thought they were American and the rest of the world hadn't a clue. They just thought they were under attack!

It took some time before all of them realized that they were not of this Earth! Or perhaps not of this physical dimension. They could outrun anything we had at the time. (Anything we have at the time of this writing, for that matter.) The rounds fired upon them would mostly miss their target and the rest would not penetrate the hull of their ship. If the UFOs were picked up on radar, most of the time they were gone before the fighters could reach their position. But gone where? Solid objects were returned on radar and would remain, either in motion or stationary for several minutes. On the next sweep, there was either nothing or the bogeys were at an impossible altitude. Then nothing!

In many cases, eyewitnesses confirmed the radar's readings. Reliable witnesses like police officers, commercial and military pilots, professional people and the average John and Mary Doe. A complete cross-section of the public at large.

Once the military acknowledged the futility of the attacks, they curtailed them. Now they will scramble fighters on rare occasions, only to escort the unknowns out of the area.

But the government and military will not easily admit defeat. If, however, the phenomenon doesn't exist, then there never was an attack. Thus, no defeat. But rest assured that the government is still working on the alien problem. And by some reports . . . with them!

One can hardly criticize the government's position on the matter. If you recall the 1938 radio broadcast of "The War of The Worlds," it is easy to see that, faced with the unknown, most people will panic. Having just emerged from World War II, the public would be certain that we were under attack. This time not by conventional weaponry but against technology centuries more advanced than our own. What chance would we stand against such a formidable foe?

Wall Street was still living under the shadow of a depression, lifted only by the war. Such a revelation would plunge it right back in.

The mission of the U.S. Air Force is to defend our air space against domestic and foreign enemies. How could they admit that to do so was impossible in this instance?

How could mankind admit that he was no longer "king of the hill"? Mankind, hitherto, was the most advanced species in the universe. Mentally, morally, physically and technologically. God's chosen people! In fact, the only life forms in the universe existed on mother Earth. To suggest otherwise would be heresy! To *prove* otherwise would be mortifying!

Fundamentalists feel that "if it isn't in the Bible, it doesn't exist." "God would have told us if there was life elsewhere in the universe." "If we were made in God's image, how could an intelligent race, that looked different from us, exist?" And when all else failed, the old stand-by, "it's the work of the devil!"

Then in 1970, Erik Von Daniken published his best-selling book, "Chariots of The Gods?" and much irrefutable evidence was brought to bare. Evidence that threatened to shake the world's religions to their very foundations!

Chapter 2

In 1970, Erik Von Daniken published a book entitled "Chariots of The Gods?" It was based upon his work in archaeology all over the world. The main theme of this work was that flying machines, commanded by intelligent beings, have been reported all over the world since prehistory. This finding was something that mainstream archaeologists had remained silent about or refused to accept. Rock carvings in Egypt, Peru and the Americas carried strange accounts of visitors from the sky. Some were clad in "diving-suit-like" garb, reminiscent of the twentieth century space suit. There were other figures of small humanoids with large black eyes (typical of the small greys reported by alleged alien abductees from around the world today). There was also an exacting carving of a man in the cockpit of a flying machine complete with control panels.

Archaeologists would explain these figures as mythical gods whom these people worshipped. The problem with this theory is that these pictures were discovered all over the world. Different peoples - different cultures and customs - same phenomena!

All of these ancient artists had a couple of things in common, however: They had the ability to reproduce the likeness of people, animals and inanimate objects with great skill. They also left an exact record of things that they actually witnessed to depict their culture and lifestyle for future generations. Could it be that they threw in a little science fiction just for fun? And if so, how did these diverse peoples, separated by great oceans and land masses, who could not speak the same language, come up with the same fictitious tales?

Even the folklore of the different tribes of the world echo the same underlying theme. Gods descending from the sky in mystical vehicles of fire and smoke to set moral standards for mankind and aid in their development. Folklore that jibes with the rock paintings and carvings. Folklore that is disconnected by geographical location, yet is in complete harmony in content.

The great pyramid of Giza in Egypt was reportedly built by 100,000 soldiers from the army of King Khufu. The blocks of the pyramid weigh from two and a half to fifteen tons each and are connected from the inside by "dog-bone-shaped" steel couplings. These steel locks would have to be smelted on the site or they would cool before reaching their destination and be rendered useless. These blocks were cut and stacked 450 feet high with such precision that a human hair cannot be placed between them at any point. The sides of the pyramid are aligned perfectly to true north, south, east and west. Another curious observation is that the shafts, running through its interior, are in perfect alignment with the heavenly constellation Orion.

Von Daniken cites the Ethiopian Apocalyptic writings, which state that Enoch was instructed to build the great pyramid to protect the ancient writings from an impending flood. According to the writings, Enoch garnered this revelation from the "gods from heaven" who came to him in a "flying boat" from the sky!

Most UFO abductees have reported that, during their abduction, the alien visitors warn them of great catastrophic events that await the Earth in the near future. They cite the fact that humans are polluting the Earth and its waters with waste material and depleting the ozone layer. Of course, what the "near future" is to them, compared to our assessment of time, is anyone's guess.

With the advanced technology of the twenty-first century, today's engineers are unable to duplicate the pyramids found around the world and are stymied as to how they were constructed.

In the temple of Dendera, in southern Egypt, a hieroglyph was discovered depicting two men carrying a huge "light bulb." The light bulb is attached to a cord that leads to a jar that acted as a socket. We were aware of the fact that the ancient Egyptians were capable of making glass for many things, including decorative items - but a *light bulb*?! (Fig. 1)

Daniken built a model of the light bulb according to the specifications found in the temple. A ceramic jar filled with acidic fluid acted as a battery to which the cable was connected. Electricity registered on a modern voltage meter and the bulb illuminated! (Fig. 2)

This would go a long way in explaining how the ancient Egyptians were able to see deep down beneath the earth to paint hieroglyphs on the walls of tombs without leaving scorch marks on the walls or ceilings from torches.

In the Peruvian spurs of the Andes, high on the side of a mountain, is an intricate pattern of parallel lines gouged into the earth. Other lines crisscross these lines and some run to a dead end. They are known as the Nazca lines. They were constructed by the ancients but were discovered from the air. One cannot see the pattern it forms while on the ground. Thus, its construction could only have been directed from the air.

Are the Nazca lines ancient roads? Leading to where? Dead ends at the mountain top? Or was the purpose of their construction to be used as an airport or landing strip for the "gods"? If so, who supervised their construction? And from what vantage point?

Many such mountainside figures have been discovered in Peru. On the cliffs of the Bay of Pisco, there is a three-branched candlestick formation that stands 820 feet high. There is one of a bird, one of a monkey, one of a spider, and one of a humanoid being with big black eyes. All of these formations are constructed to exact proportion. None can be discerned except from the air.

Admiral Piri Reis, of the Turkish Navy, discovered maps of the world and ancient charts while in various sea ports. During a sea battle, in 1513, the admiral captured an enemy sailor who bragged about sailing with Columbus on his voyage to the new world. Reis asked the prisoner how Columbus knew that there was land across the ocean. He was told that Columbus had a map and that the pilot still had it. When Admiral Reis came into possession of this map, he was able to compile a complete world map by using it in conjunction with the other maps and charts in his collection.

In 1929 the Piri Reis maps were discovered by a group of historians in the Palace of Topkapi in Constantinople. The maps accurately showed the coastal lines on North and South America. It also included precise data of Antarctica and the southern polar continent, supposedly not discovered until 1818.

Arlington T. Mallerey, an authority on ancient maps, eventually came into possession of the Piri Reis maps. Although he found them to be geographically accurate, the data on the edges of the map were not in the correct position. Mallerey made a grid of the map and transferred it onto a globe. The topographic data matched perfectly.

Pictures of the Earth from space also match the Piri Reis

maps. The center of the picture is directly under the lense, so the topographic data is exact. The further away from the center, the more distorted the data becomes due to the curvature of the Earth. This indicates that the Piri Reis maps could only have been made from a great height.

The maps represented Greenland as two separate islands. The seismic sounding of a French polar expedition shows that an ice bridge between the *two* islands of Greenland makes up its mass. Hitherto, Greenland was thought to be one land mass. Therefore, the ancient map could have only been made before the ice bridge was formed.

Seismic soundings also revealed mountains and valleys beneath the ice caps of Antarctica that matched the maps perfectly. Even the coast line of Antarctica, that has been hidden by ice since before man supposedly walked the Earth, was represented on the map. Not until the invention of the seismograph were we able to detect its true contour. It is precisely the same contour as represented on the Piri Reis maps.

In 1543, Copernicus suggested that the Earth was not the center of the solar system. In 1610 this theory was confirmed by Galileo with the aid of his telescope. Although the Sumerians, whose civilization existed as early as 3000 B.C., had already depicted a complete solar system, with the Sun, not the Earth, at its center.

Saturn was discovered by Christina Huygens in 1659. Yet an Assyrian clay tablet shows the solar system with Saturn in its proper position - complete with rings!

While on the subject of maps and charts, it would be apropos to mention the Betty Hill star map. Those familiar with ufology know that the Betty and Barney Hill incident was the first *documented* alien abduction case. The full account of the encounter was revealed in the book "The Interrupted Journey" by John G. Fuller. (Dell publishing Co., N.Y., 1966.) The star map she drew from memory, while under a posthypnotic suggestion, lends credence to the authenticity of the incident. But let's start from the beginning:

On September 19, 1961, Betty and Barney Hill were driving home through the White Mountains of New Hampshire, when they saw what they first thought was a bright star in the sky. Then the "star" began to move across the sky and closer to them. They pulled off the road to observe it more carefully. Barney took out a pair of binoculars and watched it draw within 200 yards of him. It was a disk-shaped object 60 to 80 feet in diameter. A double row of windows surrounded the disk and he could see strange looking humanoids looking back at him from inside the craft. Barney became agitated and apprehensive. To the best of his conscious recollection, he ran back to the car and sped off.

The next thing they recalled was continuing their drive home. The strange thing was that they were 35 miles further down the road than they last remembered. There was an unidentified beeping sound emanating from the trunk of their car.

When they finally reached their home in Portsmouth, New Hampshire, they realized that, although they had only stopped for a few minutes to view the curious object, the trip had taken two hours longer than it should have. Feeling exhausted and unwell, they retired for the night.

The next morning they discovered scuff marks on the tops of Barney's shoes. Betty began having recurring nightmares of being abducted and physically examined. Barney had developed an unexplainable rash in his groin area. The Hill's family physician was unable to help either one of them, so he referred them to Dr. Benjamin Simon, a prominent Boston psychiatrist. In weekly visits, Dr. Simon worked with the Hills independently for more than three months. In which time, it was revealed through the use of hypnosis, the Hills were abducted by this humanoid crew, taken aboard their craft and subjected to physical examinations in separate rooms.

The aliens communicated with them telepathically. They had told them not to be afraid - that they would not hurt them. They just wanted to examine them. Barney recalled having an instrument put around his groin. Betty related a painful process of having a needle inserted into her navel. They had told her that it was a pregnancy test. She argued that there was no such test for pregnancy but her objections fell on deaf ears. A few years later a test called amniocentesis was developed, which is a similar procedure. Also a procedure known as "laparoscopy" has been developed whereby an optical attachment is inserted into the patient's umbilical region to explore the female organs as well as to extract ova from the ovaries.

Betty recalled asking the one who seemed to be the leader of this expedition where they were from. He asked her what she knew about astrology and she admitted that she knew very little. He showed her a "star map" and pointed out their home planet in relation to Earth. Dr. Simon gave her a posthypnotic suggestion to draw the map from memory later - but only if she was able to remember it accurately. Betty was able to recreate this map in a crude two- dimensional drawing and presented it to the doctor.

The drawing was given to a Marjorie Fish, a school teacher and amateur astronomer. Fish made more than twenty three-dimensional models of the map using beads on strings to represent planets and suns. She determined the planets, indicated by Betty Hill, to be the planets around the stars Zata 1 and 2 Reticulli. However, after studying the models for several months, she was unable to determine a pattern that matched the Hill map. Prior to 1968, science was uncertain about star patterns greater than twenty light years from Earth.

In 1968 new data came out in "Gliese Catalog of Nearby Stars." This data afforded Fish more accurate information for stars up to fifty-four light years from our Sun. Armed with this updated information, she constructed new 3D models. This time she was able to correlate all stars in the Hill map to real stars in the sky. Her findings were compared to computer tests that confirmed the fact that Betty Hill, with virtually no knowledge of astronomy, drew an accurate map of a sector of the heavens thirty-seven light years from Earth, years before astronomers knew their exact location!

There were fifteen stars shown on Betty Hill's map. All fifteen are basically like our Sun, to include the possibility of planets revolving around them. It was later discovered that all fifteen stars are the only sun-like stars within that volume of space. The probability of a random map that includes all sun-like stars, with planets capable of supporting life, is less than one in ten thousand.

Maps of the Earth. Maps of the stars. Presented to the world long before the discovery of their accuracy. Maps that are later confirmed by the use of advancing technology. What is the connection? Chance? Coincidence? Were such incidences isolated, I would tend to say "yes." However, the overwhelming volume of evidence suggests that a civilization, far more advanced than our own, has and is visiting this tiny ball of mud we call Earth. The solar system of Zata Reticulli, for example, is billions of years older than our own. Any intelligent life form that may reside there has had a huge evolutionary head start.

The orthodox religions around the world will argue that, regardless of what man's science may tell us and regardless of what the millions of "kooks" from around the world may claim to have experienced, "if it's not written in the Bible, it doesn't exist!"

This is where Erik Von Daniken opened the can of worms that is being debated yet today. Were many of the heavenly visitations, described in the Bible, actually misinterpreted UFO encounters? When Von Daniken suggested such a concept, some scientists and clergymen were up in arms. However, some of those who made the effort to investigate the evidence, were forced to agree.

Chapter 3

On the fifth day of the fourth month of the thirteenth year, I, Ezekiel the priest, son of Buzi, was living with the Jewish exiles by the Chebar River in Babylonia. The sky opened and I saw a vision of God. It was the fifth year since King Jehoiachin had been taken into exile. There in Babylonia beside the Chebar River, I heard the Lord speak to me and I felt his power.

I looked up and saw a windstorm coming from the north. Lightning was flashing from a huge cloud and the sky around it was glowing. Where the lightning was flashing, something shone like bronze. At the center of the storm I saw what looked like four living creatures in human form, but each of them had four faces and four wings. Their legs were straight and they had hoofs like those of a bull. They shone like polished bronze. In addition to their four faces and four wings, they each had four human hands, one under each wing. Two wings of each creature were spread out so that the creatures formed a square, with their wing tips touching. When they moved, they moved as a group without turning their bodies.

Each living creature had four different faces: a human face in front, a lion's face at the right, a bull's face at the left, and an eagle's face at the back. Two wings of each creature were raised so that they touched the tips of the wings of the creatures next to it and their other two wings were folded against their bodies. Each creature faced all four directions, and so the group could go wherever they wished, without having to turn.

Among the creatures there was something that looked like a blazing torch, constantly moving. The fire could blaze up and shoot out flashes of lightning. The creatures themselves darted back and forth with the speed of lightning.

As I was looking at the four creatures, I saw four wheels touching the ground, one beside each of them. All four wheels were alike; each one shone like a precious stone, and each had another wheel intersecting it at right angles, so that the wheels *could move in any of the four directions. The rims of the wheels were covered with eyes. Whenever the creatures moved the wheels moved with them, and if the creatures rose up from the earth, so did the wheels. The creatures went wherever they wished, and the wheels did exactly what the creatures did, because the creatures controlled them. So every time the creatures moved or stopped or rose in the air, the wheels did exactly the same.*

Above the heads of the creatures there was something that looked like a dome made of dazzling crystal. There under the dome stood the creatures, each stretching out two wings toward the ones next to it and covering its body with the other two wings. I heard the noise their wings made in flight; it sounded like the roar of the sea, like the noise of a huge army, like the voice of Almighty God. When they stopped flying, they folded their wings, but there was still a sound coming from above the dome over their heads.

Above the dome there was something that looked like a throne made of sapphire, and sitting on the throne was a figure that looked like a human being. The figure seemed to be shining like bronze in the middle of a fire. It shone all over with a bright light that had in it all the colors of the rainbow. This was the dazzling light which shows the presence of the Lord. (Ezekiel 1: 1 - 28)

On April 24, 1964, Lonnie Zamorra, a local police Officer for the city of Socorro, New Mexico, was in the process of pursuing a speeding car, when his attention was arrested by a large plume of fire and smoke in the distance. Thinking that there may be people in need of assistance in the fire, he aborted his pursuit and sped off in its direction.

When he arrived on the scene, much to his amazement, he found an egg-shaped craft supported by three metal legs that apparently acted as landing gear, in an open desert area. He got out of his squad car and was approaching the craft when he saw two humanoids in protective clothing at the base of the craft. They saw officer Zamorra too! The two intruders hurried back into the craft and fire and smoke billowed out from the bottom of the thing. The heat was so intense that it sent the officer running for safety behind his vehicle. The craft lifted off and darted out of sight.

Officer Zamorra radioed for assistance and shortly more officers arrived on the scene. They examined the landing site. The ground was scorched where Officer Zamorra indicated the object had touched down and the level of radioactivity was noticeably higher in that area.

It wasn't long before the military arrived and closed off the area to civilians and the media. They did their own testing of the landing site and quickly eradicated any and all trace evidence associated with the incident. Dr. J. Allen Hynek, then with the government's "Project Blue Book," was part of that investigative team. Dr. Hynek was a down-to-earth scientist who, at the time, was a staunch skeptic of all UFO reports. He later admitted that this case was the one that forced him to reconsider his previous belief that all UFO sightings could be explained.

Once Dr. Hynek refused to debunk all UFO reports and took the stance that they did indeed exist, the government relieved him of his position with "Project Blue Book" and he set out on his own fact-finding mission to prove their existence. Of course he was met with much ridicule and harassment by the government and military for his trouble. But the good doctor was undaunted in his effort and was responsible for bringing to light much evidence that would have otherwise been swept under the bureaucratic carpet.

The similarities between the two preceding documented eyewitness accounts are striking. The difference is that the latter took place in 1964 AD and the former, in 500 BC.

The verses from the book of Ezekiel were echoed in Erik Von Daniken's "Chariots of the Gods?" However, instead of having a spiritual connotation, the vision of Ezekiel was compared to a twentieth century spacecraft. In fact, a craft that surpasses the space technology of Von Daniken's day.

The former chief of the Systems Layout Branch at NASA's Marshall Space Flight Center, Josef F. Blumrich, had read the book and scoffed at such a suggestion. As with the skeptical J. Allen Hynek, Blumrich set out to prove Von Daniken wrong. As with Hynek, by earnestly investigating the matter, the weight of evidence unearthed tipped the scales in the opposite direction.

Blumrich compared the translations of six different versions of the Bible. Armed with the detailed description of Ezekiel's vision and his knowledge as an aerospace engineer, he was able to reconstruct a landing craft that closely mirrored the description given. (Fig. 3) He not only designed but patented his invention. Then he wrote "The Spaceships of Ezekiel."

In his book he gave a very detailed description of the craft. *It was egg-shaped*! The crew and commander's compartment sat above a nuclear reactor. There were four cylindrical landing legs supporting the craft, each with four helicopter blades and retractable mechanical arms. At the base of the landing legs were "hoof-shaped" metal feet for stability. The craft was able to move about on land with the aid of crisscrossed hoop wheels, allowing it to move in any direction in a smooth, unhesitating manner. Spokes were placed within the wheels for support. (Fig. 4) The commander sat above the nuclear reactor in his chair before a control panel of flashing colorful lights.

Blumrich's interpretation of Ezekiel's vision might sound like a fantastic leap from that of today's biblical scholars. But let's take the biblical text, break it down and compare.

I looked up and saw a windstorm coming from the north. Lightning was flashing from a huge cloud and the sky around it was glowing. Where the lightning was flashing, something shone like bronze. (Verse 4)

This verse is hauntingly reminiscent of my own close encounter sighting as a teenager. Although there was no windstorm connected with my sighting, there was a huge cloud of smoke illuminated from behind by glowing lights. I do not recall the lights flashing, however, most sightings include the report of flashing multicolored lights. Ezekiel and his contemporaries knew nothing of electrically powered lights or flying vehicles. So to him, what else could the lights represent except lightning? What else could such a grand vehicle be, descending from the sky, if not a chariot for God himself?!

The mention of the fact that the object "shone like bronze" indicates the recognition of a metallic surface. The time of day is not mentioned. Therefore, whether the craft was indeed constructed of bronze or the angle of the Sun gave its silver finish a golden hue, lends fuel for debate. What is not debatable is that what Ezekiel witnessed was a solid, physical object - probably metallic in its construction.

It would only seem logical that a landing craft, such as described here, would cause a great disturbance of wind in the immediate area. Ufologists agree that there are three types of propulsion used by UFOs: nuclear fission, nuclear fusion and electromagnetic.

The majority of UFOs sighted since 1947 are reported to be silent and do not display any plumes of fire being emitted from them. Most photographs of UFOs are found to have a haze around them. This fact makes skeptics highly suspicious of the authenticity of the picture. However, those that have taken the pictures, and other eyewitnesses, insist they are able to see the same halo encircling the object first hand. This phenomenon is "ionized air" caused by the electromagnetic propulsion system. In effect, the craft has made its own gravitational field onto itself. Although it is within the gravitational field of the Earth, it is not subject to its laws. This would account for the breakneck speeds and hairpin turn maneuvers reported in most UFO sightings. A pilot in a conventional aircraft, subject to the earth's gravitational field, would not survive such maneuvers.

Ezekiel's UFO did not appear to be of this type, however. I doubt, very much, if fossil fuel, as used by twentieth-century Earth spaceships, was the propellent employed by this craft, but it obviously was not electromagnetic. If Blumrich's theory is correct, it was powered by a nuclear reactor. Whichever, it was a solid, metallic vehicle that produced a great amount of wind, fire and smoke.

It may also be of interest to note that the 1st verse of "The Good News Bible" states that the *"sky opened and I saw a vision of God."* In the "American Standard Version," it states, *"the heavens were opened and I saw visions of God."*

When we think of the word "sky," we usually envision that which is within earth's atmosphere. The word "heaven," however, is thought of as that vast expanse *beyond* earth's atmosphere. Many languages do not discriminate between the two words. The German word, *"himmel,"* means both sky and heaven. So did Ezekiel see this object descending from heaven, the perceived dwelling place of God, or simply from the sky? Daniel 4: 33, speaks of the *"dew of heaven."* Jeremiah 4: 25, speaks of *"the birds of the heavens."* Neither dew nor birds are found outside of the earth's atmosphere. Therefore, it is obvious that anything above the surface of the Earth was referred to as "in the sky" or "heavens," interchangeably.

In either case, Ezekiel observed the heavens/sky "open." An odd choice of words to describe the craft's descent. Yet many UFO witnesses describe the craft entering their view from a "hole" in the sky. As if the sky had been punctured to allow the craft to enter the earth's environment. Some will say, "the sky opened up like a great page being turned in a book." Some liken it to a curtain opening. In the case of my sighting, the smoke, at the outset of the event, seemed to be pouring out from one point in the sky. Although, because of the billowing smoke, I was unable to view a "hole" in the sky.

Is this phenomenon evidence of the UFOs entering our physical plane through another dimension? *Are* they from another dimension? Or are they from another planet traveling through another dimension? Could the answer to all of these questions be "yes" at the same time?

Perhaps later chapters will lend credence to this possibility!

At the center of the storm I saw what looked like four living creatures in human form, but each of them had four faces and four wings. Their legs were straight and they had hoofs like those of a bull. They shone like polished bronze. In addition to their four faces and four wings, they each had four human hands, one under each wing. Two wings of each creature were spread out so that the creatures formed a square, with their wing tips touching. When they moved, they moved as a group without turning their bodies.

Each living creature had four different faces: a human face in front, a lion's face at the right, a bull's face at the left, and an eagle's face at the back. Two wings of each creature were raised so that they touched the tips of the wings of the creatures next to it and their other two wings were folded against their bodies. Each creature faced all four directions, and so the group could go wherever they wished, without having to turn. (Verses 5 - 12)

The American Standard Version (verse 5) reads, "*And out of the midst thereof came the likeness of four living creatures.*" Here Ezekiel "likens" the four objects to living creatures. He does not state that they *are* living creatures. Once again, being unfamiliar with the technology that he is witnessing, he can only compare what he is experiencing to objects with which he is familiar.

Once again Ezekiel refers to the metallic surface that "*shone like polished bronze.*" This time he is referring specifically to the legs of the craft. In Blumrich's concept of Ezekiel's spaceship, the landing gear would definitely resemble a living being. Especially if there were recognizable faces at the top of the cylindrical objects.

The Apollo spaceship had US flags around it. Four of them, to be exact. Many such craft have displayed the American eagle. Airplanes are decorated with decals of flags, animals, people and other images. What is particularly intriguing is the fact that the faces, displayed on Ezekiel's craft, were of creatures indigenous to Earth.

Marc Davenport, in his book "Visitors From Time," suggests that UFOs are time machines from our own future. This might explain the images of four Earth creatures on a craft far beyond the time of Ezekiel. Another dimensional craft might be another explanation. Whichever, there the faces were, surrounding the landing legs, confronting our biblical hero.

The feet of the landing gear resembled the hoofs of a bull. (The American Standard Version uses the word "*calf.*") The lunar module had rounded plates at the bottom of the landing legs. A round, thick plate, like a bull's hoof, would serve the purpose of stability and prevent the legs from sinking into the surface on which it rested. (Fig. 5)

Mechanical arms with hands positioned on the landing legs would enable the occupants to retrieve samples off the planet's surface without having to disembark the craft. Mechanical hands were employed by the Mars land rover to gather rock samples.

The wings that Ezekiel observed were helicopter blades. As he observed, there were four of them on each leg. They would collapse downward while not in use and could be activated for the purpose of flight within the earth's atmosphere. As the blades rotated, the craft would levitate off the ground. When the rotations of the blades were slowed, the craft would settle back down and the "wings" would fold down to their sides. Certainly the craft could move in any direction, rise from the ground and descend, without moving their "bodies," as it was all one solid unit.

Among the creatures there was something that looked like a blazing torch, constantly moving. The fire would blaze up and shoot out flashes of lightning. The creatures themselves darted back and forth with the speed of lightning. (Verse 13-14)

The fire that was being emitted from the nuclear reactor was necessarily in the middle of the four landing legs. I would suspect the lightning that was witnessed was static electricity arcing between the landing legs.

As I was looking at the four creatures, I saw four wheels touching the ground, one beside each of them. All four wheels were alike; each one shone like a precious stone, and each had another wheel intersecting it at right angles, so that the wheels could move in any of the four directions. The rims of the wheels were covered with eyes. Whenever the creatures moved, the wheels moved with them, and if the creatures rose up from the earth, so did the wheels. The creatures went wherever they wished, and the wheels did exactly what the creatures did, because the creatures controlled them. So every time the creatures moved or stopped or rose in the air, the wheels did exactly the same. (Verse 15-21)

Figure 4, depicting the "wheel within a wheel," is pretty much self-explanatory. A wheel of this design at the base of each landing leg would afford the craft universal movement while on land without having to stop, turn or change direction. The spokes within the wheel acted as supports. The artist seemed to paint the "eyes" around the rim of the wheel as a design. Perhaps they served a more functional purpose. Perhaps they were the ends of the spokes that had been inserted into the rims of the wheel.

Many ufologists have likened Ezekiel's "wheel within a wheel" to the typical saucer shaped UFO. Blumrich's explanation, however, precisely depicts Ezekiel's observations as stated in the Bible, without taking it out of context.

Here again, Ezekiel is fascinated by the fact that the wheels would move to and fro, up and down with the body of the vehicle. Being affixed to the vehicle, what choice would they have?

Above the heads of the creatures there was something that looked like a dome made of dazzling crystal. There under the dome stood the creatures, each stretching out two wings toward the ones next to it and covering its body with the other two wings. I heard the noise their wings made in flight; it sounded like the roar of the sea, like the noise of a huge army, like the voice of Almighty God. When they stopped flying, they folded their wings, but there was still a sound coming from above the dome over their heads. (Verse 22 - 25)

Here, Ezekiel attempts to convey the sound of the rotors in

flight. Never having heard the sound of a helicopter rotor before, he could only compare the din to "the roar of the sea," or "the noise of a huge army." He also notes that when the craft stops flying and settles back to the ground, the blades collapse to the sides of the landing legs. In the absence of the sound of the rotors, he can still hear the hum from the nuclear reactor of the landing module.

Above the dome there was something that looked like a throne made of sapphire, and sitting on the throne was a figure that looked like a human being. The figure seemed to be shining like bronze in the middle of a fire. It shone all over with a bright light that had in it all the colors of the rainbow. This was the dazzling light which shows the presence of the Lord. (Verse 26 - 28)

Above the nuclear reactor was the command module. The commander sits in the commander's chair in front of the control panel. The flashing multicolor lights from the control panel, reflecting off the commander and all within the module, would indeed display a spectacular light show to Ezekiel's eyes.

The occupants were decidedly human. They picked Ezekiel up (abducted) and took him for a ride in this fantastic vehicle. Ezekiel recognized the occupants as human and states as much. They were not of the short grey species that is most often reported by modern day abductees. However, some do report humans commanding twentieth century UFOs. Such reports primarily come from the British Isles. They are referred to as "Nordics." They are human in appearance. The males are tall, muscular and handsome. The females are also tall and beautiful. Most, if not all, have long blond hair, typical of the Nordic countries.

The occupants spoke to Ezekiel in his own language. This is a leap of faith if we are to assume that they were extraterrestrial. However, all alien abductees claim that the occupants speak to them telepathically, regardless of their physical appearance. Could it be possible that Ezekiel's aliens spoke to him within his mind and the thoughts were translated there for his comprehension? Not being familiar with the process, all he knew was that he understood what they were trying to communicate to him.

Blumrich also suggests that there was a "mother ship" involved. This would orbit the Earth while the landing craft separated from it, descending to the Earth, to accomplish its mission. Personally, I feel that he was thinking along the lines of his time. This was the manner in which the lunar landings were accomplished. It is the phrase, "the sky opened" that leads me to believe that the craft entered earth's atmosphere through a vortex from another dimension. Even if the visitors were extraterrestrial, quantum physics dictates that such a phenomenon is possible by bending space-time. This would also answer any objections to the length of time it would demand to traverse from one galaxy to another.

If Ezekiel's vision was the only biblical passage that could be compared to a modern day UFO, it could be dismissed as coincidence. However, the Bible is full of such correlations.

Chapter 4

The Israelites left Sukkath and camped at Etham on the edge of the desert. During the day the Lord went in front of them in a pillar of cloud to show the way, and during the night he went in front of them in a pillar of fire to give them light, so that they could travel night and day. The pillar of cloud was always in front of the people during the day, and the pillar of fire at night. (Exodus 13: 20 - 22)

Perhaps the largest multiple witness sighting case of unidentified aerial phenomena was that of the exodus of the Israelites from bondage out of Egypt. Moses had been "chosen" by the Lord to free the slaves from Egypt's grasp. He had been told how to accomplish this mission by a voice coming from a "burning bush." Moses noted that the bush was burning yet it was not consumed.

There the angel of the Lord appeared to him as a flame coming from the midst of a bush. Moses saw that the bush was on fire but that it was not burning up. (Exodus 3: 2)

The modern interpretation of the burning bush is just that - a small bush on fire. The Hebrew word "bush" actually means a "thicket" or "group of bushes." Similar to the British interpretation of "bush," which is "woods" or a "clump of trees." Imagine the glowing, blinking lights of a landed UFO in the "midst" of a thicket. Having no concept of the principle of electric lights, and your line of sight is on the other side of the thicket from the object, it might appear that the thicket was on fire, yet the foliage does not burn up. Moses decides at this point to approach the phenomenon. As he does so, a voice from the midst of the "fire" speaks to him, telling him not to come any closer. (Exodus 3: 5) The reason given was that Moses was on holy ground. Could it be that the occupants of the UFO were aware of the danger to Moses should he come within close proximity of the craft?

On December 29, 1980, Betty Cash, a café owner, her

employee, Vickie Landrum and Vickie's grandson, Colby, were driving along a narrow, deserted road near Huffman, Texas. The time was approximately 9:00 P.M. They spotted an intense light, several miles ahead, hovering over the tree tops. They soon lost sight of it. Then, without warning the object settled down in front of them over the road. Betty hit the brakes. It was a huge, diamond-shaped craft. It was brightly illuminated and emitting a great amount of heat.

The car became unbearably hot, due to the intense heat from the craft. The two women opened the car doors and got out to escape the heat within. Vickie quickly returned to the car, however, to calm her frantic grandson. Betty, on the other hand, decided to get a better look at this technological marvel. She shielded her eyes as best she could and drew closer. She was exposed to the heat for several minutes.

To add to the bizarre events of that evening, military helicopters came on the scene and the UFO retreated. Betty and Vickie reported up to twenty-three helicopters in the area that night, chasing off the curious craft. Many other people in the area substantiated the women's story by reporting having seen the helicopters and the UFO in the sky on that evening.

Later that same evening, all three of them began displaying signs of medical problems. Betty Cash especially demonstrated severe discomfort. She developed a headache that only worsened as the evening progressed. Her skin reddened as if exposed to the Sun for an excessive amount of time. Water blisters appeared on her head and face.

By the next morning she was so ill that she could not get out of bed. A few days later she was admitted to a local hospital where she was treated as a burn patient. She spent two weeks in the hospital and was released.

One week later she was readmitted as her condition had worsened. She continued having violent headaches and had lost most of her hair. A skin condition had developed as a result of the burns and she suffered from diarrhea and vomiting.

Betty's mother came to Texas to take her daughter home with her to Birmingham, AL. There, Betty was hospitalized and properly diagnosed with radioactive poisoning.

With the assistance of the Mutual UFO Network, (MUFON) Betty Cash and Vickie Landrum tried to get answers from the military as to exactly what it was that they encountered that fateful night in Texas. Their requests for information were either ignored or answered with bureaucratic double-talk. Either way, the military has steadfastly denied any involvement with the incident.

Betty Cash's legal and medical battles lasted for eighteen years. She died from her physical ailments on December 29, 1998. Ironically, it was on the 18th anniversary of the UFO encounter.

The Cash - Landrum incident is just one example of many such unfortunate close proximity encounters with UFOs. All too many individuals have suffered severe burns or radiation poisoning after an encounter.

Whether or not this was the reason for the warning from the "burning bush" remains to be seen. The fact remains that Moses was told to come no closer. If this was indeed an extraterrestrial craft, the occupants would already be aware of the fact that earth's inhabitants revered them as gods. They could use this knowledge to assure man's adherence to their explicit instructions, and to retain the alliance of the Israelites to accomplish their mission. That mission being, to end the enslavement of one group of the species by another. Again, the intent of these celestial visitors, as in the case of Ezekiel, seemed to be to dictate social and moral standards to a primitive race.

Once the Pharaoh of Egypt released the Israelites from bondage, they had set out across the desert for the "promised land." At that time they had no idea where they were going but had faith that Moses would lead them - because God would lead Moses.

True to his word, God appeared to them in the sky as a "pillar of cloud by day and a pillar of fire by night." The Bible is not specific as to whether this pillar was horizontal or vertical in the sky, however, it was emphatically stated that the pillar-shaped object was camouflaged by a cloud during the day and was well illuminated at night.

Outside of the common saucer-shaped UFOs, one of the more common shapes reported, in the twentieth century, is the "cigar-shaped" craft. These have been seen traveling in both the horizontal and vertical position. They often are surrounded by a cloud of smoke, especially during daytime sightings, and are well illuminated at night. Skeptics brush these sightings off as dirigibles. However, this explanation would not account for the smoke, unless it was in deep trouble. The lights on these crafts are nowhere near FAA regulation. A dirigible is a slow-moving airship. Cigar-shaped UFOs have been reported to hover for a time, then dart out of sight. Furthermore, if a dirigible takes a vertical position while aloft, get out of it's way, because it will not stay aloft for long.

Of course, cigars were nonexistent in Moses' day, so a pillar or column was the only artifact with which they could relate this aerial marvel.

For forty years this pillar-shaped UFO went before the Israelites, guiding their way through the desert. However, not long after they had begun their trek, Pharaoh had a change of heart. He believed that he had made a mistake by emancipating his slaves and ordered his army to retrieve them. (Exodus 14: 5 - 9)

Pharaoh and his army caught up with the Israelites by the Red Sea. Then, when the Egyptians were about to overtake the Israelites, the UFO moved from in front of them to their rear to separate them from their pursuers. Pharaoh's army was halted by a wall of smoke, while the UFO provided light for the Israelites. (Exodus 14: 19 - 20)

Moses held out his hand over the sea, and the Lord drove the sea back with a strong east wind. It blew all night and turned the sea into dry land. The water was divided. And the Israelites went through the sea on dry ground, with walls of water on both sides. (Exodus 14: 21 -22)

When UFOs have been reported over water, witnesses have observed a disturbance in the water directly below the craft. It is as if a strong air flow is attempting to displace the water beneath it. Often observers, directly under a UFO, will report feeling "weighted down," as if the gravitational pull of the Earth has increased and it is harder to stand or walk in that area. They feel confused and disoriented. Ufologists believe that this is due to the anti-gravitation device employed, which afford these crafts their unmatched maneuverability.

If the "pillar" has positioned itself over the water and has activated this device, a strong enough force could be directed onto the surface to literally displace the water in its path right down to the seabed. Of course, such a thrust against the Earth might well propel the craft upward, unless there was an opposing anti-G force above the craft to create a counter balance.

One would naturally expect the seabed to be deep mire, once it was exposed. However, the Bible clearly states that the seabed was "dry ground." Not even a strong east wind that blows all night long would cause the seabed to be hard, dry ground by morning. A wind strong enough to part the water and dry up the mud beneath it, would probably be strong enough to blow the Israelites and Pharaoh's army back to Egypt! It is more probable that this same anti-G force, that parted the water, continued its downward pressure until the water in the seabed had been squeezed out like a sponge.

This accomplished, the anti-G beam could be removed from the path it had created and be concentrated on the water walls on either side. The Bible attributes the parting of the waters to a "strong east wind," yet the waters remained parted as the Israelites made their escape through the path created by it. Once again, such a wind would not allow anyone to walk through it. There seemed to be no pressure on the fleeing Israelites as they walked the path. Therefore, the anti-G force was obviously removed from that area.

And the Egyptians pursued, and went in after them into the midst of the sea, all Pharaoh's horses, his chariots, and his horsemen. And it came to pass in the morning watch, that Jehovah looked forth upon the host of the Egyptians through the pillar of fire and of cloud, and discomfited the host of the Egyptians. And he took off their chariot wheels, and they drove them heavily, so that the Egyptians said, "let us flee from the face of Israel, for Jehovah fighteth for them against the Egyptians." (Exodus 14: 23 - 25)

At this point, Pharaoh orders his army into the sea to pursue the Israelites. There is still a path of hard, dry ground to support the weight of the men and their chariots. Once the army is between the water walls, the object above them causes them to be "discomfited." "Discomfited" is the term used in the American Standard Version. The Good News Version uses the phrase, "threw them into a panic." Discomfited - panicked - confused - disoriented: All such terms are used when referring to the physical effect of witnesses while in the close proximity of the anti-G force of a UFO.

This force was not being applied while the Israelites were fleeing through the Red Sea. Now that they were safely on the other side, the force moved from the water walls and the pressure was being felt by the Egyptians. So much so that the wheels of their chariots were being driven down into the seabed and breaking off.

Now Moses holds out his arms toward the sea as a signal to release the force completely. The anti-G force is switched off and the water walls collapse in on Pharaoh's army.

If there was any doubt before, it is clear at this point that the occupants of the UFO are working in concert with Moses to free the Israelites.

The "pillar of fire and cloud" remained with the Israelites throughout their journey through the desert until they reached the "promised land." After they had crossed the Red Sea, there is even more dramatic evidence of a technologically superior race at work.

In Exodus 25: 10 - 22, Moses is given detailed instructions (far too detailed to relate here) for the construction of the Ark of the Covenant. The instructions are to the very inch. Moses is told what material with which to build it and where the staves and rings are to be fitted. A complete blueprint was verbally given for its construction, with warning not to deviate from them.

In further verses, other items, such as a table, lamp stand, tent and an altar were ordered to be fabricated with specific instructions, right down to the type and color of clothing and footwear to be worn.

Moses was told that the Lord would speak to him in the "tent." (Exodus 33: 7 - 11) Here he could speak to God and hear God's voice. However, Moses was told that he could not see the face of God or he would die. Moses was also warned that no one was to come close to the Ark or they would also be killed.

In 2 Samuel 6: 1 - 7, we find that Uzzah and Ahio are transporting the Ark on a cart to Jerusalem. The oxen stumbled and Uzzah, thinking the Ark might fall, reached out and touched the Ark. He fell dead on the spot!

Erik Von Daniken, in his "Chariots of The Gods," discovered that if the Ark were built today, according to the specific instructions given to Moses, it would be an electric conductor capable of producing and storing several hundred volts. Furthermore, the "tent" would act as a loudspeaker. Obviously this was used for two-way communication.

Why would God need a device for two-way communication? What purpose would there be for an electronic conductor to people of Moses' time? What happened to the Ark of the Covenant?

Where is it today? These mysteries, though thought provoking, are secondary to the question of, "what exactly was the pillar of fire and cloud?" The picture painted in this book certainly doesn't parallel the Cecil B. DeMille version. However, if one compares the actual text of the Bible with the aforementioned hypotheses, taking into consideration what is known about modern UFOs, Mr. DeMille's treatment of the exodus becomes strictly Hollywood.

The pillar of fire and cloud was thought to contain the spirit of the Lord. This aerial phenomenon is mentioned throughout the old and new testaments. It soon came to be referred to as simply, "the cloud," "the spirit of the Lord" or "the glory of the Lord."

As Aaron spoke to the whole community, they turned toward the desert and suddenly the dazzling light of the Lord appeared in a cloud. (Exodus 16: 10)

"I will come to you in a thick cloud." (Exodus 19: 9)

All of Mount Sinai was covered with smoke, because the Lord had come down on it in fire. (Exodus 19: 18)

But the people continued to stand a long way off, and only Moses went near the dark cloud where God was. (Exodus 20: 21)

Moses went up Mount Sinai, and a cloud covered it. The dazzling light of the Lord's presence came down on the mountain. To the Israelites the light looked like a fire burning on top of the mountain. The cloud covered the mountain for six days and on the seventh day the Lord called to Moses from the cloud. Moses went on up the mountain into the cloud. There he stayed for forty days and nights. (Exodus 24: 15 - 18)

During all their wanderings they could see the cloud of the Lord's presence over the tent during the day and a fire burning above it during the night. (Exodus 40: 38)

As the priests were leaving the temple, it was suddenly filled with a cloud shining with the dazzling light of the Lord's presence and they could not go back in to perform their duties. (1 Kings 8: 11)

I looked again and this time I saw a scroll flying through the air. The angel asked me what I saw, I answered, "A scroll flying through the air; it is thirty feet long and fifteen feet wide."
(Zechariah 5: 1 - 2)

Prepare a way for him who rides on the clouds. (Psalm 68: 4)

And build your home on the waters above. You use the clouds as your chariot and ride on the wings of the wind. (Psalm 104: 3)

(see Fig. 6)

Chapter 5

Anyone who thinks that there is not enough evidence to prove the existence of UFOs, has simply not studied the evidence. There is far too much documented evidence in existence to present in this volume. Since the advent of the camcorder, photographic evidence has grown dramatically.

Skeptics are quick to conclude that visual effects or overlaying pictures on film, easily explain these videos as hoaxes. They fail to take into account the fact that highly technical and very expensive equipment is required to produce such a fake. Most of the home videos taken of UFOs are by people who are lucky to be able to afford a camcorder let alone the equipment necessary to pull off such a hoax. All UFO footage is subjected to rigorous scrutiny by qualified technicians. Sometimes hoaxes *are* discovered. This is actually advantageous to UFO researchers, as it helps them to distinguish hoaxes from authentic photographic evidence.

In 1950, when visual effects equipment was unheard of , a McMinville, Oregon farmer, Paul Trent, grabbed his camera and was able to take two pictures of a low flying saucer-shaped object over his property before it darted out of sight. These pictures were taken with 110 film. The film was submitted to authorities in an effort to identify the object. The farmer was never paid for the pictures or his testimony. He had nothing to gain from perpetrating a hoax, except the unrelenting ridicule of his peers. These pictures have been examined and reexamined since they were taken. Experts have yet to offer a conventional explanation for the object in the print.

All too many times an honest citizen will take a video or still frames of a UFO and naively hand them over to the Air Force to be analyzed. The paper trail will end there. The evidence seems to vanish into thin air. No one seems to have a clue as to the whereabouts of the pictures. In fact, they may deny having ever accepting receipt of the items.

Then there are those videos that never find their way to that crack in the system. In the early 1990's, a camera crew was filming a music video in Red Square when the crowd witnessing the event began to point skyward. The camera operator pointed his camera in the direction of their attention just in time to catch a UFO hovering above them. It began moving slowly, then darted out of sight. No official explanation was ever given. No plausible official explanation is ever given (with the exception of obvious misidentifications), only official denial.

Dr. Richard Haines, a retired NASA scientist, has collected more than 3,500 cases of pilot sightings from around the world. This is quite an accomplishment, given both civilian and military pilots usually refuse to discuss UFO sightings for fear of losing their jobs. Most pilot sightings are multiple witness sightings due to the very nature of their situation. Almost always there are a copilot and/or crew aboard that are able to confirm the details of the event. In the case of commercial flights, some of the passengers witness the object. Often other aircraft in the area will radio in their confirmation of the unknown craft. In most cases, ground radar is able to track and record the movements of the target.

Invariably there is an official investigation. Invariably someone in high authority will show up to collect the radar reports and witness' testimony and to inform all parties concerned, on no uncertain terms, that this is a "nonevent." It never happened!

Ted Philips, a UFO researcher has collected more than 4,400 "trace evidence" cases from 65 countries. Trace evidence is physical evidence of a UFO landing site. In most of these cases there have been witnesses to the landings. About 25% of the reported landings involve witnesses having seen humanoid beings exiting and reentering the craft.

All of these landing sites have several common characteristics. There is a scorched round depression in the ground where the craft was said to have landed. Often there are four small round depressions (landing pods) around the center ring. The ring is usually ten to fifteen feet in diameter. All four landing pod depressions will measure the same distance from the edge of the center ring and from one pod depression to the other. The color, texture and properties of the soil in the affected area will have changed from that of the soil surrounding the ring. The "ring" soil will not absorb moisture. It will not support seed germination. Radiation levels are higher in the ring area than that of the surrounding soil. These altered properties in the ring area are not just on the surface but will generally go about fourteen feet down.

The United States government has claimed that they have stopped collecting any documentation pertaining to UFOs since the mid 1960's. Timothy Good, in his book "Above Top Secret," presents a melange of allegedly leaked top-secret documents that prove the government has been, and is presently, investigating the UFO problem.

Stanton Friedman, a nuclear physicist and UFO researcher from Canada, petitioned the Air Force for declassified material concerning the subject under the "Freedom of Information Act." After a long court battle, he received many documents that were mostly "blacked out." Their excuse for this was, "in the interest of national security."

Here we have the military telling us that UFOs do not exist. Thus, they are not a threat to national security. They claim that it is such a nonissue that they haven't documented cases on the subject since the 1960's. Then, after a long court battle, they begrudgingly turn documents over to the public on the subject dating from the mid 1940's to present day. However, the documents, for all intents and purposes, are worthless. They have been rendered unreadable. Why? "National security!" . . . .
. . . I'm confused!

If UFOs, that do not exist, are classified Top Secret, then what is the Easter Bunny? Perhaps . . . Confidential?

Some people say, "there couldn't possibly be life in outer space." I would ask them to remember that *we are in outer space.* Our tiny planet is on the edge of an obscure spiral galaxy - one of countless billions in the known universe. It rotates on its axis at the speed of 1,070 miles per hour, while hurling through space at a rate of 67,000 miles per hour. It travels 1,608,000 miles per day. The only thing that keeps it from flying off into the cosmos is the magnetic pull of a comparatively small star that we call the Sun.

Creationists dismiss the "big bang theory" as the explanation for the creation of the universe. Yet, the Bible, though it states that God created heaven and Earth in six days, never mentioned the method used in that creation. Is it possible that both theories are correct? Saint Thomas Aquinas, one of the most revered figures in Catholicism, when men of science first attempted to break through the wall of ignorance in the dark ages, stated that "reason and faith could coexist."

Imagine taking an apple and removing the core. Place an M-80 firecracker into the hole. Place it in the middle of the room, light the fuse and stand back. Bits and pieces of that apple would scatter about the room. Now go to one small piece of apple over in the corner. Concentrate on that bit of apple and nothing else. After a time you will find life forming on it. The longer you focus your concentration on that bit of apple, the more life you will witness evolving on it. After a substantial period of time has elapsed, two facts will become apparent; That bit of apple will not only be teeming with life but it will be the only object of your attention.

If you are able to tear your attention away from that corner of the room and think for a minute, you will realize that there are other bits and pieces of apple scattered everywhere. All of those pieces are matter from the same original source. All scattered to their present resting places by the same force. All subject to the same environment. If you were to walk across the room to the farthest point from your bit of apple, it would not be surprising to find another bit of apple also teeming with life.

"But even if there is intelligent life somewhere out there, the distances are so great! How can they get from their world to ours within their lifetime?"

Quantum physicists acknowledge the fact that space can be bent. In doing so it creates a "wormhole" through which one can enter at their point in space and come out at a predetermined point in space anywhere in the universe. (The term "wormhole," used in this context, has not been borrowed from science fiction. It is the other way around.) Our scientists have not yet been able to harness the mechanics of this procedure for practical use but who is to say that one day they won't? Who is to say that a more advanced civilization hasn't already done so?

There was a point in time when science realized that electricity existed but, until Benjamin Franklin flew his kite in a thunder storm, there was no known method for harnessing it for practical use. Today, splitting atoms is the preferred method of producing electricity. We flick on a light switch a hundred times a day without giving "old Ben" as much as a thought.

If these galactic visitors are employing this "wormhole" to create a vortex through which they may traverse the vast expanse of the universe, it would go a long way in explaining three factors associated with UFO sightings:

How they can get from their world to ours and back again within their lifetime.

The seeming ability to "pop" in and out of sight.

The much repeated observation of the "sky opening." (The mouth of the vortex opening to allow them entrance into our gravitational field.)

It would also prove that the visitors do not travel through space per se, but through another *dimension*.

What does the Bible say about other dimensions? What does Jesus Christ himself have to say on the matter? Does He spell it out for us or must we read between the lines? Or perhaps there have been some lines removed by the orthodox church because they didn't complement conventional wisdom.

Let's examine that!

PART TWO

JESUS OF NAZARETH AND THE SPIRITUAL REALM

Chapter 6

"The kingdom of God is within your midst." (Luke 17: 21)

"Within your midst" are the words used in the King James' version. *"Within you"* are the words used in the American Standard and Good News versions. On the surface it would appear that these two phrases mean the same thing. However, "within you" would seem to indicate that heaven is within each individual's body - the soul. "Within your midst" means, "in the middle of" or "amongst you."

Did the revision from the King James' version attempt to clarify Jesus' message? Or was it that "within your midst" did not jibe with the church's concept of heaven's location being up in the sky? After all, God's chariots of fire, pillars of cloud and flying scrolls all came down from the sky. The logic of their day would dictate that the sky must be heaven's locale. That must be where the spirit goes upon its departure from the physical form. It would only confuse the masses to think that heaven was right here in their midst.

In 2 Corinthians 4: 18, Paul speaks of the "seen" and the "unseen" worlds. *For we fix our attention, not on things that are seen, but on things that are unseen. What can be seen lasts only for a time, but what cannot be seen lasts forever.*

Look about the room in which you are presently sitting. Can you see the pictures that are being broadcast over every cable channel available? They are there! I can prove it. Just turn on the cable TV and there they are!

Listen carefully. Can you hear your favorite radio station? It's there. Just turn on the radio and your favorite music springs to life.

Where were all these sights and sounds before you activated the necessary device to see or hear them? Were they out in the cosmos somewhere just waiting for you to reach out and drag them into your living room? Not at all. Every television program, radio show, shortwave broadcast, CB frequency and on and on, that can be picked up by any device designed for their purpose, is "*within your midst*" at this very moment.

Our senses operate within a given frequency limit. These limits are considered normal. A radio station will broadcast a program at a frequency modulation that is outside our normal range of perception. Your radio is simply a device that receives that frequency and translates it into a frequency that our human ears can perceive. The same is true in the case of television, not only on an audible, but visual level.

At the beginning of the twentieth century, we believed that anything that could not be seen or heard simply did not exist. Such logic is understandable under the concept that the human range of perception is all-inclusive. However, for thousands of years man has acknowledged the fact that lower animals exhibit a wider range of perception than man.

When I was in grammar school, my grandmother had a dog whistle for the purpose of calling her dog from the back door without yelling like a banshee. I would use the whistle on occasion to call the dog. When I did, I heard a very shrill tone. After a while I mentioned this fact to my grandmother. She informed me that people can't hear a dog whistle. It was out of the range of human hearing. I blew the whistle for her and she insisted that all she heard was wind. This confused me because I was certain that I could detect a sharp high-pitched tone. Then again, Grandma was the authority. Who was I to argue?

Not long afterwards, I had a professional hearing test. The doctor informed my parents that I was able to hear tones that only a dog could hear. I had been vindicated!

As the years went on, I have lost that ability. When a dog whistle is blown, I hear only wind. Yet, when my auditory fibers were younger and more plentiful, I was able to personally confirm the fact that sounds exist on a frequency beyond that of the average human auditory range. Should you have any doubt, just blow a dog whistle on any residential street and see how many dogs confirm it for you.

On several occasions it has been proven to me that the visual range of a dog is wider than our own.

My Uncle Harry and Aunt Augusta, whom we lovingly referred to as Aunt Gusty, lived in Flint, Michigan. Their son, nicknamed "Bud," resided in a nearby suburb. Aunt Gusty passed away one sad day and Uncle Harry insisted that, on the evening of her death, she returned to the house and spent the night with him. According to him, her visits were frequent and welcomed. I recall my mother commenting to my dad about the poor old man's "hallucinations." He was alone now, after all those years, and was in shock.

Not long after Gusty's death, Uncle Harry and Bud came to visit us in Detroit one evening. We had a cocker spaniel at the time named Lady. She was a gentle and loving creature who would make friends with anyone who paid her some attention. Of course she would bark when anyone rang the doorbell but, after a family member would allow them into the house, she knew that all was well. After a quick once-over sniffing, it was time to play.

The doorbell rang and Lady began protecting the house with a resounding bark. As soon as we let them in, however, she just wanted to sniff them out. Normal greetings were exchanged between them and my parents and they took a seat in the living room. Lady first went over to Bud who was sitting on the sofa. According to Lady, all was fine with him. Then she went over to Uncle Harry, who was sitting by himself in an overstuffed chair. Immediately she began to bark frantically. The hair on the back of her neck stood straight up. I was sitting to his right, so I could see the direction of Lady's gaze. She was looking at the wall directly above his head! My father began yelling at her to "shut up." Unheeding, she continued to bark wildly at the wall above Harry's head.

My mother had to scoop her up and put her outside. Harry and Bud exchanged a knowing smile, as my father, dumbfounded by the dog's reaction, apologized for the scene.

Later that evening, while our guests were still there, my mother decided to give Lady a second chance and let her in. Oblivious to anyone else's presence, she ran over to Uncle Harry's chair and repeated the ritual. Once again, staring right past his head at the wall. Mom put her out again and didn't let her back in until they had left.

Anyone who owns a dog quickly becomes quite familiar with its temperament. I can assure you that Lady was just that - a lady. A gentle, docile creature. With Lady, friends were always welcomed and strangers did not remain that way for long. She had never reacted in that manner toward anyone before this incident nor after. Then again, it wasn't Uncle Harry she was reacting to. The entire family witnessed her reactions twice that night. She was barking at something behind him that was outside the vibratory range of our sight.

I was first married in 1966 to a young woman who had an abnormal fear of virtually anything she didn't understand. This, of course, made our relationship interesting, given my propensity to metaphysics and UFOs.

We bought our first house in Detroit, only two blocks away from my parents' home, in the spring of 1968. We owned a dog that we had named "Buck." His mother was a German Shepherd and his father was "well respected in the neighborhood." We had acquired Buck as a puppy and now he was a little more than one year old. Once again, we knew his temperament and what to expect from him. I was working the afternoon shift at the time. One day my wife calmly informed me that we had a ghost in the house. Her nonchalant air concerning such a revelation was totally out of character for her. Skeptically, I asked her what made her think so. She told me that she could feel a presence on occasion accompanied by "cold spots." She also reported that the dog would act strangely at these times. I had never felt any such presence in the house but decided to reserve an opinion at that time.

Not long afterwards, I was home of an evening. I was in the kitchen with my wife, when Buck, in the living room, began to bark frantically. I hurried into the living room to see what could be wrong. Buck was looking up at a blank wall. The hair on the back of his neck stood straight up (shades of Lady) as he continued to bark. Then, unexpectedly, he jumped back as though someone had taken a swing at him. He recovered quickly and returned to sniff the floor and wall in the area that was, only a moment before, the object of his agitation.

Though strange behavior on Buck's part, I reasoned that it may have been a shadow on the wall that had caught his eye and let the matter rest. A few days after that, I was again home in the evening. I was sitting on the living room floor assembling some massive wooden project. What, exactly, I can't recall. Just one of those things that assured me that there was "some assembly required." Buck was lying on the floor across from me. My wife was sitting on the couch, sewing. "Our ghost is back," she calmly advised me.

"How can you tell?" I asked.

"I can feel the cold all around me," she said.

I looked at Buck who was lying still but his eyes were firmly fixed upon my wife. I wasn't more than three feet from her and I could feel nothing. I kept my eyes on Buck and said, "If there is a spirit in this room please come over to me." His eyes moved slowly from my wife to me. Immediately I felt cold air engulf me. "I can feel it!" I told her. "Watch Buck's eyes. Okay, spirit, now go back to my wife."

The dog's gaze moved back to my wife. "I can feel it again," she said. The cold spot had just left me.

Then it became a game. Perhaps a dozen times I would ask the spirit to move to me. Then I would ask it to go back to her. The cold spot obeyed each time. Each time we would confirm to the other that we either had felt the presence, or that it had departed. Each time Buck's eyes moved to where I had asked the spirit to go.

Obviously Buck had come to terms with our spectral house guest. It did not seem malicious or threatening. Perhaps that is why my wife was not fearful of its presence. Regardless, my wife and I knew it was there "within our midst," and Buck confirmed it.

Dogs also have an uncanny sense of impending death. Their manner of demonstrating it can prove quite unnerving.

My grandmother was diagnosed with lung cancer in 1976. The doctor assured the family that it was the type that would spread quickly and spare her from a lingering death. Given there was nothing more they could do to cure the disease, she asked not to be hospitalized. She went to her deathbed, in her Detroit home not far from ours, in May of that year. There she laid until the strongest eighty-five-year-old heart her doctor had ever seen refused to continue functioning in October.

I went to visit her one evening before she died. It was still warm enough outside that her bedroom window was open. She slept peacefully while I listened to about five dogs, in the immediate area, howling their eerie lament. Though I stayed for only an hour or so, my mother, who had moved in to help my grandfather with her, later told me that the dogs howled for about three solid hours. It was as if their owners were indifferent to the din. Perhaps they had brought their dogs in and others were let out. Regardless, the dogs howled unceasingly for hours that evening. Two days later Grandma was gone.

In researching this book, I consulted with my sister, Ann, to make certain that I had my facts and dates straight. While doing so, she related a story about my grandfather that I either hadn't been aware of or had forgotten. After my grandmother's death, my grandfather moved in with my parents. One year later he became bedridden and remained so for three years. One night a dog sat outside his bedroom window and howled for about thirty minutes. Two days later Grandpa began choking. An ambulance was summoned and he was rushed to the hospital. Two weeks later he joined Grandma in that dimension we refer to as "heaven."

In 1997 my mother was seventy-nine. She and my sister, both widowed, shared a ground floor apartment in Westland, Michigan. Mom was finding it increasingly difficult to walk, to the point that a wheelchair was employed when leaving the house. Other than that, she was in fairly good physical condition for a person of her years.

She underwent in-home physical therapy to strengthen her legs. Her goal was to be able to walk into her church without having to be wheeled in. By the end of January it became apparent that the therapy was successful and she was overjoyed when she walked into church of her own accord on the 9th of February.

On the following Wednesday, mom was sitting in her living room when a dog came to the door-wall, looked in at her and began to howl. This disconcerting chant soon aggravated her and she closed the blinds. This did not deter the dog in its efforts to drive the message home. The howling persisted. She asked my sister to get rid of the howling menace. My sister went to the back porch and was finally successful in chasing the dog off.

Two days later Mother had a massive heart attack. She was rushed to the hospital where she died and was revived three times. An emergency operation was performed to remove the blockage and she was put on life support. By Sunday morning her condition had worsened to the point that the only thing keeping her body functioning was the machine. My sister and I reluctantly gave permission to suspend life support measures. She passed over in peace.

As in the case of my grandfather, if it wasn't for medical intervention, she would have died exactly two days after the incident with the howling dog. It would seem that my mother's side of the family is cursed with howling dogs as a harbinger of death. As strange as it may seem, however, there have been many such canine messengers reported . . . and have been since recorded history.

Some people report that a bird will fly into a closed window shortly before the death of a family member. One woman told me that her grandmother and mother knew of the impending death of a loved one by the appearance of a little boy. A child in a stocking cap would come up to a window and peer into the house. Each time they would rush outside to find the lad gone. Each time a family member would die within a couple of days. Whether or not this phenomenon continued with her is unknown.

Are all of the aforementioned cases coincidence? Could everyone, who has reported such incidents, be hallucinating? Or is it possible that, like radio and TV frequencies, the spiritual realm is right here "in our midst". . . albeit out of our vibratory range? That when conditions are ripe, that dimension "bleeds" through to ours?

Have you ever been listening to a radio station and hear another station gradually creep in over the first? My present wife and I live in a condominium complex. We had a portable TV set in our upstairs bedroom a few years ago. When we would have the set on CBS and our next door neighbor (who has since moved) was talking on his cordless phone, the audio on our TV would cut out and every word he said on his phone came in loud and clear. When the other party was speaking, the TV's audio resumed but our neighbor's end of the conversation was perfectly audible over the TV's speakers.

I had a grade school teacher who lived near Detroit's Metropolitan Airport. One day he told the class that, the previous night, he was listening to a record playing on his "hi-fi" when the music was interrupted by a pilot hailing the control tower for permission to land.

A man in Chicago, several years ago, had gone to the dentist for a filling. Immediately afterwards he began hearing faint music and voices in his head. He thought he was losing his mind! After visiting several doctors, it was discovered that the filling in his tooth was touching a nerve and acting like a crystal set. The frequency from a nearby radio station was being picked up and transmitted to his auditory senses twenty four hours a day. Unable to turn down the volume or change the channel, the filling was removed.

Anyone who accepts the concept of the human soul and it's departure from the physical body upon death, already accepts the concept of another dimension. If two dimensions can coexist at the same time, in the same space, why not three? Why not three hundred - three thousand - three billion? We have come to accept the fact that this is the case with radio and television frequencies but the human soul is quite another matter. Perhaps it is due to the fact that science has only recently acknowledged the existence of an energy force that permeates all living things. Perhaps, if science takes that discovery one step further, the huge rift between science and religion will lessen

Chapter 7

1 Corinthians 15: 44 refers to the spiritual body being within the physical, as do many passages. People of all faiths need no convincing of this fact. However, science demands that any such claims be studied and measured under strict laboratory conditions. When it comes to the human soul, which cannot be put under a microscope, once again, reason and faith come to a parting of the ways.

In the 1930's, a Russian technician, Semyon D. Kirlian, stumbled upon the technique of photographing the energy field that envelops all living things. While repairing hospital equipment, he discovered that the interaction of electric currents and photographic plates produced the imprint of living organisms on film. The process that came to be known as the "Kirlian effect" was developed by him and his wife in 1939.

It wasn't until the late 1940's that Russian scientists began serious research with Kirlian photography. Then, in the 1970's, the United States realized its potential and began research of their own. By 1975 the University of California at Los Angeles was able to measure auras with great accuracy. The process employs a metal plate and a generator that will produce a high voltage field of variable pulse and frequency. The film and the organism to be photographed are placed in contact with the plate. Light is not used in this process. The result is a striking photograph of a multicolored corona surrounding the organism, commonly referred to as an "aura."

The human aura will display brilliant, shimmering spikes of light emanating from the physical body. This technique has been found useful as a diagnostic tool. Disease will show up as a disturbed flare pattern, in the affected area of the body, long before the disease is advanced enough to be clinically diagnosed.

The aura's flare pattern can be altered by weather, cosmic disturbances (such as solar flares), a meditative or agitated state, day or night, mood shifts, health condition or sexual excitement.

In short, this electromagnetic field, which emanates from all living things, constantly changes with the subject's environment and emotional state.

If you subject a leaf to Kirlian photography, its aura will display itself around its entire perimeter. Cut that leaf in half and the "phantom" of the missing half will still appear on the photograph. Likewise, if a person's limb has been amputated, that missing limb will still appear on the film. However, if a corpse is subjected to the same process, the aura is conspicuously absent.

Could this electromagnetic energy field be a part of that "unseen world" referred to by Paul in his letter to the Corinthians? Is Kirlian photography the device which translates light waves that are beyond our normal senses, into the range of our perception? Is this fiery aura the "smoking gun" that proves the soul's existence? The fact that it is present in the living and absent from the dead, confirms the fact that it is responsible for animating the physical form. What becomes of this energy field upon its departure from the physical form?

Science acknowledges this energy field because it can be measured and studied under laboratory conditions. Science also states that energy cannot be destroyed . . . it can change form, but it cannot be destroyed. Yet, when confronted with the question of the human soul, they refuse to admit to its existence. They have no scientific proof of the soul's continuance after physical death. Therefore, their official position is that this particular energy mass simply "winks out" upon physical death.

There are many people in the world who claim to have the ability to see auras without the use of scientific devices. Ruth Montgomery, Jean Dixon, and Char Margolis are just three of the well-known names, out of thousands of self-proclaimed psychics, whose optical and auditory ranges are outside that of the norm.

Ruth Montgomery, who lived on a farm as a young girl, claimed that she could see the spirit of a chicken depart its body when its head was chopped off. Char Margolis speaks of seeing and hearing spirits as a young girl. I have spoken with several psychics who have made similar statements. One lovely lady, residing in a suburb of Detroit, whom I discovered to be an excellent sensitive, recalls being punished for her gift. She was about seven when she told her mother something pertaining to her grandfather (long-deceased) that there was no earthly way she could have known. Her mother asked her how she knew about this, to which the little girl replied, "because your father just told me. He is standing right next to you."

The young girl was severely scolded and sent to bed without dinner. She learned quickly that such a talent was not acceptable and kept further revelations to herself. It wasn't until reaching adolescence that she realized this was a God-given gift. If she would mentally wrap herself in light, pray that God would allow in only benevolent spirits, and trust in her spirit guides, she could use this gift to God's glory.

Although psychic ability has become more widely understood and accepted as fact in recent years, it has long been tabooed by orthodox Christianity as the "work of the devil." The common theory behind this belief is that only Jesus could commune with angels or disembodied spirits. However, in John 14:12, Jesus tells us that whoever shall believe in Him and His works shall also do such works. (And even greater works than Himself.) Granted there are far too many charlatans in the world, and those who would use such a gift for evil purposes. But is it so surprising, given Jesus' promise, that some of God's children possess this gift and use it benevolently?

Frequently there are reports of the ability of the dying to glance into that dimension referred to as "the other side," shortly before passing over. Most doctors will explain away these reports as wishful thinking or hallucinations, either drug-induced or resulting from the lack of oxygen to a dying brain. However, consider the case of my cousin's husband, Steve:

My cousin had left for work early one morning. Steve was dressing for work himself when he succumbed to a brain aneurysm. He passed out on the hardwood bedroom floor wearing only his undershorts. There he remained until his wife returned from work to find him. She summoned an ambulance and Steve was rushed to the hospital, where an emergency operation was performed to remove the pressure on the brain.

Although the operation was successful, he had developed pneumonia due to exposure from lying, unclad, on the floor all day. The doctors made a valiant, week-long effort to cure him. Meanwhile, unbeknownst to Steve, his father was on *his* deathbed in Florida. It was decided not to tell Steve's father about his son's failing condition in Michigan. Consequently, neither man knew of the other's impending death.

At 3:50 P.M. EST, one Tuesday afternoon, Steve died in Michigan. At 4:10 P.M. EST, in Florida, Steve's father turned to those at his bedside and announced, "I have to go now. Steve is waiting for me at *the door*." And he passed away.

My beloved maternal grandmother was a strict orthodox Christian from the old school. "When you die, your spirit goes up to heaven and your body goes into the ground. On Judgment Day, Jesus will come down, open your grave, bring you back to life and you will live forever." This is the wonderfully simplistic teaching I received as a child from Grandma.

At the young age of sixteen, I had already been investigating metaphysics for some time and believed it possible to communicate with disembodied spirits on some level. I asked Grandma for a favor: "If it is possible," I said, "when you die, come back and knock on the walls, so I know it's you."

"But it's not possible," she assured me.

"But if it is,"

"But it's not!"

"But if it is," I persisted.

"All right," she finally agreed just to shut me up, "if it's possible, I'll come back and knock on the walls." The pact was forged.

As the years passed, I had all but forgotten about our agreement. I grew up, got married, served two years in the Army and was back home for seven years before my grandmother died. My grandfather had moved in with my parents immediately afterwards and his house was sold. All of the furnishings had been removed by late November. On the night of the twenty-ninth of November, I had an "out of body experience." (Although, for me, OBEs are quite infrequent, I am able to distinguish them from a fanciful dream. This phenomenon will be discussed in a later chapter.)

I found myself in my grandparent's home. Although I was not present when the furnishings were removed, in my OBE there were no furnishings in the house - just as it actually existed at the time. I walked down the hall to the back bedroom where Grandma had drawn her last breath. I stopped outside her room and looked in. There she was as I last remember seeing her in life. Sickly, drawn and haggard. She had been reduced to skin and bone by the ravages of the disease. She came toward me with outstretched arms. As much as I cared for my grandmother, I was repelled by her appearance and pushed her away. She approached me again and again I thwarted her advance.

"You're scaring him, Florence." I heard a woman's voice say. I looked to my left to see a stern but gentle middle-aged woman standing in the hallway with me. I somehow recognized this person but could not place her. I looked back into the room and watched as my grandmother transformed herself into the lovely, elderly lady that I knew and loved before the cancer had claimed her body.

This time, when she approached, I threw my arms around her and held her close. "David," she said, "I can't get out of the house. They came and took everything away but they've left me and I can't get out."

"Grandma, you're dead." I informed her.

"Oh no, I'm not!" she insisted, unwilling to accept such a concept, given she knew that she was very much alive and aware.

I walked her down the hall and into the living room. "You are in spirit now. You can walk right through that wall."

"No, I can't!" she persisted.

"Grandpa is living at Mom's now. Don't you want to be with him?" I said, attempting to arouse her incentive to try.

"Yes,"

"Then just walk through the wall. Go ahead. You can walk right through the wall."

She thought about it momentarily, then cautiously approached the living room wall. When she made contact with it, she bounced off, staggered backward and fell to the floor. "Grandma!" I cried out and knelt down beside her dazed and confused form. I had momentarily forgotten that she couldn't have hurt herself. Yet, the shock of the incident snapped me back into my physical body three miles away.

I awoke with a shock, unable to move for a couple of minutes. When normal feelings resumed in my body, I was able to think clearly. Grandma was trapped in the house! She was unaware of her present circumstances and, even though I felt there was a loved one with her for condolence, she was unable to cope with the situation and move on. I had tried to help her on *her* level of existence and failed miserably. Now I felt obligated to try again from the physical side.

It was November thirtieth and the house keys were to be

53

handed over to the real estate agent the next day. There was no procrastinating to be done. I had to visit the house that day. I went to my mother and told her about my "dream" of the previous night. I told her that I wanted the house key so I could try to talk Grandma into leaving before the house was sold. Of course Mom dismissed my "dream" as nothing more than that but, if it would ease my mind, she was willing to play along. She handed me the key.

I walked into the little two-bedroom house, which had been part of my life for the past twenty-eight years, for the last time that late afternoon. Though this was the first time in my life that I had seen it without furnishings, it looked exactly as I had seen it the night before - in spirit. I went straight to Grandma's bedroom. The faint scent of the perfume she always wore still lingered. I couldn't tell you the name of the product but the odor, when mixed with her body chemistry, was as unique to her as a fingerprint. I stood in the middle of the barren room and spoke to the walls, which answered only in echoes.

"Grandma, I know that you are here and that you can hear me," I began. "I understand that everything is confusing to you now but you must believe me. You have died. Your physical body is dead and buried. You are aware of your surroundings because your spirit lives on and always will. You think that you are trapped in this house but, in fact, you are more free now than you have ever been. Look up and you will see a light. Go into the light. Everyone, who has gone before you, is there. They are waiting for you. It's the way out. Jesus is the light and the light is the way. Go into the light."

I spent perhaps forty minutes praying and talking to her. It was starting to get dark and the electricity had been disconnected, so I decided to wrap it up. As I was leaving, just in case she was still in the house, I opened the front door wide and told her that this was her last chance to get out. She would feel that she could leave in this familiar manner, if she wasn't yet convinced that walking through walls was a viable possibility.

That night my wife and I slept soundly as the season's first snowfall lightly coated the ground. Our two-year-old and three-month-old sons were fast asleep in the next room. Of course Buck guarded the premises by sleeping at the foot of our bed. At 3:00 A.M., four or five loud, resounding bangs startled us into consciousness. Buck began barking frantically. He didn't head for the door though, as was his custom when someone would knock. He stood barking and looking around, as if unable to locate the source of the disturbance. I jumped up and ran to the front door. No one there! I went around the house, looking out each window. Nothing. I checked on the boys. They remained asleep.

I checked the clock and began cursing the late night prankster. My wife convinced me to try to go back to sleep. Buck had quieted down and all was well, so I returned to bed. I had lain there, in an agitated state, for about ten minutes, when, **bang . . . bang . . . bang . . . bang!** Buck started barking again. Being fully awake now, I was able to understand the dog's confusion. The pounding had no single source. It seemed to be resonating throughout the very structure of the house.

I was out of the bed at the first "bang" and "bark." I ran to the front door, then repeated the rounds of the house with as much speed as I could muster.

There was simply no one out there!

Now I was angry! I had to calm Buck down again and check on the boys, who were still unfazed be the ruckus. I used all the dirty words I knew and half of them that I didn't. Who could be pounding on the walls at this time of night? Where was their location?

After a long discussion with my wife, I reluctantly went back to bed. I got up a couple of times to look outside, hoping to catch the trouble makers in the act. Around 5:00 A.M., I finally lost consciousness and slept, undisturbed, the rest of the night.

The next morning, I threw on my clothes and a coat and went out to examine the grounds around the house. The snow had begun falling around 11:00 P.M., so there would have to be footprints of the culprit somewhere. When I had completed two rounds of the perimeter without finding any other footprints than my own, it hit me . . . Grandma! I remembered the pact we had made so many years before. Obviously, so did she.

I had felt two inches tall for having cursed the source of the pounding that night. I recall hoping that she had knocked on the walls and ran away, so she couldn't hear my tirade. It would seem, however, that she didn't hold it against me. A couple weeks later, I was at work as a tool and die apprentice for the Ford Motor Company in Dearborn. At that time there were no women working at that facility. Out of the blue, I was overwhelmed by the fragrance of perfume. Not just any perfume - it was that unique scent that identified only one person. Not only was there the fragrance but I could sense a presence that I had come to know and love over the entire length of my short life.

I was working in an area by myself, so there was no possibility of the scent belonging to anyone else. I looked all around for a possible source of the odor. I found nothing. I called a fellow worker over to my area and asked him if he smelled anything. He sniffed the air. "Yeah, perfume. Is that you?" He said, half joking.

I smiled. "No," I assured him, "that's my grandmother. She has come to say 'good-bye'."

Chapter 8

I was drafted into the U.S. Army in May of 1969. Though the Viet Nam conflict was at its apex at the time, I was fortunate enough to draw overseas duty in Germany. I was stationed near a small town called Zweibrucken (literal translation, "two bridges"). After only a couple of months in country, I rented a flat in town and had my wife join me.

Due to the comparatively high price of real estate in Germany, it is a common tradition that a family will buy or build their home, live in the upper level and rent out the lower. Then when the eldest son marries, he will rent the lower until the parents are gone, then move to the upper and rent out the lower. This arrangement assures the fact that a given home will remain in the family for many generations. It would seem that some family members are stubbornly reluctant to give up the rights to their property - even after death.

Working at a small Army post is akin to living in a small town. Everybody quickly gets to know everybody else - and their business. My interest in the paranormal was widely known around post. One day a sergeant Emerson (pseudonym) came to me and asked for my help. He explained that he and another sergeant at the post, shared a two-bedroom flat in town. Normally they were both down-to-earth men who had, heretofore, never believed in such things as ghosts. However, over the past few months, their opinions were being changed for them by a series of unexplained occurrences in their dwelling.

They rode to work and returned home in the same vehicle every day. Yet, sometimes they would return to find certain items moved from one spot to another. At first they attributed it to absentmindedness on one or both of their parts. They started to pay closer attention to the layout of the flat and where they had left certain belongings. The incidents persisted.

The building was heated by an oil-burning furnace in the living room. On several occasions they would both witness the oil shoot into the air and onto the carpeting. When the landlord examined the furnace, on more than one occasion, they were informed that it was functioning properly. They could often feel a presence or cold spots in the room.

One evening they had invited a friend over after work. As the friend, who had never been to their place before, walked through the door, he began yelling, "Get out! Don't you see him? He's right there!" Needless to say, the man ran to his car and was gone before Emerson and his roommate could say a word.

The next day at work, Emerson confronted the man for an explanation. "I'm sorry," he told the confused sergeant, "I just couldn't stay. You may not believe me but all of my life I have seen the spirits of dead people. I can't go into a funeral home because the ghost of the deceased is always at their own funeral. I just can't handle it! But I'm telling you, there is one in your house!"

Unfortunately, this gentleman had rotated back to the states so I was unable to question him personally.

"So I wonder if you could just come over and see what you think." Emerson asked of me. I told him that I was not a professional exorcist - just an interested amateur. He said that was fine. (I think he meant "better than nothing.") So I agreed.

I knew my wife wouldn't want anything to do with an evening of "ghost chasing," so one evening it was arranged that we and another couple, Sergeant Teague and his wife, would visit Emerson at his home - just to meet new friends. We devoted an hour or so to small talk, then the subject of Emerson's ghost "innocently" came up.

The girls remained in the living room as Emerson and his roommate took Teague and me on a tour of the flat. I had no particularly uneasy feelings in any of the rooms. "Let's go into the bathroom," Emerson suggested, "sometimes we will feel it the strongest in there."

I walked in first, turned right around and literally shoved the three men aside to get out. "It's there!" I declared, as a strong sense of foreboding hit me as I walked through the doorway.

When we returned to the living room, both girls were in tears and asking to leave. We made our apologies - though they assured us that they well understood - and left.

The next day I told Emerson that Teague and I would return one night to conduct a seance. I had never done so in my life, but my curiosity had piqued now and twenty-two seemed like a fine age to start.

As promised, Teague and I returned one cold night in the winter of 1971. The oil furnace was working perfectly and the entire flat was comfortably warm. Sergeant Emerson's roommate had rotated back to the states, so that left the three of us alone in the flat to conduct the seance. I walked around to each room before we began. Once again, I didn't experience any uneasy feelings - not even in the bathroom. But then, I am not a sensitive.

I asked Emerson to place a card table in the center of the living room. Two candles were placed in the middle of the table and lighted. We brought in three wooden chairs from the kitchen, which was adjacent to the living room and took our seats around the table. We joined hands. I told them that, no matter what happened, not to break contact with each other.

I began by saying a prayer. (From what I had read on the subject, it was the proper and safest thing to do.) That done, I addressed the entity in the house. "If there is a spirit in this house, please make your presence known." My request was met with silence. The candles' flames burned steadily. I made the request again. Again, nothing. I spoke to the walls in what little German I had learned while in country. That received as much response as English.

For a good half hour we tried to acquire some form of evidence that verified the presence of an apparition to no avail. Emerson said, "Sometimes I'll feel it in the kitchen. Should we try in there?"

I wasn't about to relocate the table and chairs to another room and start all over again, but I agreed to the three of us moving into the kitchen as a last-ditch effort. "Don't break contact with each other." I reminded them. "Hold hands and get up together, slowly." We had barely raised off our seats when the candles' steady flames "winked" out in unison. We sat back down.

The only light afforded to us now was a small electric nightlight, eerily shining from the kitchen. Now we found it necessary to break contact to relight the candles. After doing so, we tried repeating the motions that may have blown the candles out. They burned steadily. We exaggerated our motions by getting up quickly, flapping our arms and even blowing in the direction of the candles. Their flames barely flickered.

We decided to try getting up again and moving to the kitchen. The candle incident had given us renewed hope. This time we were successful in retreating to the next room without the candles being affected. There was an open archway separating the two rooms. As we walked into the kitchen, we found it just as warm as the living room. Once again, I began summoning the spirit. After only ten minutes of non-response, we agreed to return to the living room.

The instant we walked through the archway, we were greeted by a chilling cold. The temperature in the living room had dropped about twenty-five degrees in the short ten minutes we were in the adjacent room. Yet, the oil furnace in the room continued to put out its heat. "What do you feel?" I asked Emerson.

"It's cold!" he said softly.

"What do you feel?" I asked Teague.

"I feel it too. Cold!"

"Me too," I confirmed their observation. We stepped back into the kitchen for comparison. It was just as warm there as it was a moment earlier. It was as if an invisible door held the cold air inside one room without affecting the other. We moved in unison to the table and took our seats around the glowing candles. Now that we had confirmed the presence of the entity and were certain that we had its attention, it was time to send it on its way.

"I am speaking to the spirit in this room." I continued. "You are no longer physically alive. You have died and your spirit is free to go where it chooses. You no longer have to remain in this house. Look up and you will see a light. Go into the light. Your loved ones are waiting for you there. Go into the light."

I clumsily repeated the previous lines in German. "Go into the light" was easy. The rest - I could only hope spirit could grasp the gist of. We sat in amazement as the room steadily warmed to its previous temperature. I said a final prayer and ended the session.

It was about three months after Teague and I had left Emerson's home that evening, that I happened to run into him on post. I was quick to ask him about the success of the seance. He was happy to report that there had been no disturbing incidents after that night. I was relieved, not only for Emerson but for the spirit of one lost soul who appeared to be unaware of his circumstances and was, at long last, at rest.

My father passed away on Sept. 13th 1982, at the age of seventy-five. My mother sold their home and moved into a one-room apartment. After living there for about six months, my present wife, Laura, and I had taken Mom grocery shopping. On the way back to her apartment, she told us that she could feel my father's presence on occasion. She tried to dismiss this as imagination born of grief. Then she would find items of clothing in the closet had fallen to the floor after returning from an outing. Mom was always a meticulous housekeeper, making certain that everything was in its place and well secured to remain that way. After several such occurrences, she thought she had better speak to the only one in the family that might take her seriously. She had scoffed at my unconventional views concerning metaphysics in the past. Now that she was experiencing unexplained phenomena, first hand, she was searching for answers. Any port in a storm.

When we returned to her apartment, we sat three grocery bags on the kitchen table and she led us into her bedroom to see if anything had fallen to the floor in her absence. Everything was as she had left them. We discussed the matter for a few minutes, then I decided, once again, to "talk to the walls."

"Pops," I said, "if you are here, let us know by knocking something over. Nothing that will break - just something that will show us that you are here."

No sooner had I spoke the words, when we heard a thud in the kitchen. The three of us hurried back to the kitchen to find one of the bags of groceries had fallen off the table onto the floor. We asked each other who had placed that particular bag on the table. Perhaps it was left dangling off the edge. We examined the bag to find that it was filled with paper products . . . nothing that would break. A package of toilet tissue was on the bottom, making it flat and well balanced. If it was not set fully on the table top, it would have fallen immediately. The bag in question had been placed there fifteen minutes before it toppled.

Momentarily, I thought of repeating the ritual I had performed in Germany and with my grandmother, but I caught myself. I figured that Pops was here for my mother's sake. He was watching over her and waiting for her to join him. It was not my place to send him on his way just yet.

This incident is far from proof of my father's continued existence. However, in the summer of 1985, another incident occurred that convinced me that my dad was still near to lend a helping hand in times of need.

Laura's son from a previous marriage, Rob, was at that rebellious age of fifteen. One day he decided to run away from home with an eighteen-year-old friend of his. Of course the police were notified but they had more pressing business than to look for a couple of teenagers who had voluntarily made themselves invisible. The parents of the other boy were used to him taking a hiatus. Besides, he was eighteen and legally on his own.

Several times my wife had asked me to go find him, knowing full well that it was an impossible chore. After the third day of wondering as to her minor son's whereabouts, she was beside herself with worry. Having had enough of the situation, I told her that I was going out to find Rob and I wasn't going to return without him.

Here it is around 9:30 P.M., already dark, Rob could be virtually anywhere and I'm driving aimlessly down a dark street wondering where I was going to sleep that night. I asked myself where a couple of young men might be at such an hour and headed for the local Burger King. The restaurant was two miles from our home in Trenton, Michigan, a downriver community south of Detroit. When I arrived, I drove around the parking lot and looked inside the building. There was no sign of Rob or his companion.

I was exiting the parking lot when I realized the futility of this exercise. I stopped the car and said aloud, "Pops, you're going to have to help me. I can't go home without him. Please, show me where he is."

I sat still for a minute, then turned right onto the main road. I had gone only a half mile when, for no apparent reason, my attention was directed to the Trenton Recreation Center on my right. I turned into its empty parking lot against all logic. The Center was closed and dark. There wasn't a sign of life in the area. I drove behind the building, stopped and turned off the ignition. Getting out of the car, I cautiously looked around. There was a vacant field behind the building with tall weeds. I listened and looked for signs of life as I walked down a muddy path in the field. This was foolish! This was obviously not a place for two runaways to hide out. They were probably holed up at a friend's house. I swivelled around in the mire and returned to the car.

I had almost reached my vehicle when an unexplainable force stopped me. Though I didn't hear the words, I could sense it saying, "Stand still." I obeyed for about three minutes, then logic overtook me and I took two more steps toward the car when that pesky force stopped me dead in my tracks again. "Just stand still!" it seemed to dictate. This time it wasn't so much my obedience that kept me planted as it was my inability to move. There I stood for a couple more minutes, looking around and listening. Then, as quickly as it came, the force released me. Without a second thought, I proceeded to the car, circled around the building and drove through the parking lot toward the main street.

I was halfway through the parking lot when I was forced to slam on the brakes to avoid hitting two figures that had emerged from between the trees on my right. Needless to say, it was Rob and his pal.

Had I left the lot when my logic told me to, either the first or second time, I would have just missed them. My leaving when the "force" allowed me to, placed the two boys directly in my headlights.

Was it my own sixth sense at work? Was it merely a coincidence, despite the astronomical odds? Or did my urgent plea result in my father reaching out from that unseen world, which is "within our midst," to lend a helping hand in this one?

Chapter 9

Most orthodox Christians are taught to dismiss metaphysics as either nonexistent or the "work of the devil." Most are willing to do just that - providing the cases presented to them are someone else's anecdotes. But when the phenomenon is staring them in the face, they either have to deny their own senses, as a safety mechanism, which excuses them from having to deal with the matter, or learn to incorporate this new information into their own belief system to the point where it makes sense. A prosaic solution can usually be found for most seemingly unexplainable mysteries. However, when one simply assigns a prosaic answer, to satisfy their apprehension, they are as a child whistling in the dark.

My sister and I were raised in the Methodist faith. Though it is obvious to the reader by now that my beliefs have strayed somewhat from that time-honored denomination, my sister has been faithful to the letter of orthodox Christianity all her life. She and I have had many long discussions on the subject of metaphysics versus the teachings of the Bible. I have always tried to use scriptures to prove my point. She will use other passages to try to disprove the same topic. Although our debates would always end in a stalemate, they made stimulating conversation.

As previously stated, my mother and Ann shared an apartment for several years. Two weeks after Mom's death, my sister was preparing a meal for one in the kitchen when she heard a spoon fall to the tile floor behind her. She turned and surveyed the floor for the utensil to find nothing. There was a spoon sitting on the counter near the source of the sound but nothing to be found on the floor. She gave the incident no further thought at the time. A few days later, the same scenario occurred in the same manner. This time she got down on the floor and examined every inch of it. No spoon!

The incident repeated itself two more times within the following week. She never did find a spoon on the floor, though she was certain she heard one fall to the floor not two feet from her. After the fourth time she purposely dropped a spoon on the floor to make sure that this was the sound she had heard. It was.

Shortly thereafter, Ann moved to a one bedroom apartment in the same complex. She was in the process of transferring her clothes from a cardboard box to her dresser in the bedroom, when she felt someone watching her. She turned to see a solid vapor form with round black eyes peeking around the corner of the doorway at her. "Oh, my God! Oh, my God," was her breathless response. The form remained for a few seconds, then retreated backward out of sight.

She did not hear the words but she had the feeling that Mom was telling her that she just wanted to make sure that she was all right in her new place. She ran to the open doorway and called out for mother to stay - but to no avail. She checked for shadows and light reflections. There was nothing that could have caused the specter. Though it was a startling experience, she was not afraid to stay alone in the apartment. The experience convinced her that mom was still around and watching over her.

My mother had a series of romance novels that she spoke highly of before her death. My sister, who worked in a one-person office, took the books in to work with her to read during her lunch periods and at slow times during the day. She read the first in the series with great enjoyment. As she finished the last page and set it down, sorry that the book had to come to an end, she looked up in amazement as a "picture" of my mother was suspended in midair in the middle of the office. The knowing smile on Mother's face was saying, "I told you those books were good."

My sister reported these incidents to me shortly after each had occurred. Knowing my interest in the paranormal, she thought that I would be able to give her a definitive answer to the mystery. I assured her, though I had read extensive volumes on the subject and related some of my personal experiences to her, that the only thing I really knew was that the phenomenon existed. It was not something to fear, but to embrace as hope for the survival of the human spirit. I could tell that these otherworldly visitations were causing great confusion in her mind. The dogmas of her faith and the reality of her own senses were on a collision course. There was no "little pigeon hole" within her brain in which to file this new material. An acceptable common denominator had to be found to integrate this unprecedented information into her belief system. Without one, she would be forced to rethink her entire world view.

I had recently read an excellent book on the subject by Bill and Judy Guggenheim, "Hello From Heaven!" Christmas was near, so I ordered a copy of the book and made her a gift of it. "Hello From Heaven" is a collection of short anecdotes from many people who have had the same type of encounter that Ann was experiencing. Even though I didn't expect it to fully explain the phenomenon, I felt it would help to assure her that, not only did it exist but that she was far from alone in experiencing it. Hopefully she would realize that she was not losing her mind and come to terms with what she believed and what she perceived.

She began reading it immediately, as if starved for the insight it might, hopefully, impart. She found that there were many people who had seen a "picture" of their loved one suspended in midair. Often a solid mist would appear in their presence. A spirit will communicate their message in thought-form instead of the spoken word. A fragrance, peculiar to the deceased, would emanate the room - similar to my own experience with Grandma.

One evening, before retiring, she read about those who were seeking confirmation of the continued existence of their loved one. They would ask the decedent to come to them in a dream or in the waking state. Often, to their amazement, the disembodied entity would do just that. Now it was my sister's turn to "talk to the walls." She said, "Mother, you always said that I snore. If I snore tonight, wake me up." Shortly thereafter, she went to bed.

Sometime during the night she was awakened by my mother's hand firmly shaking her bare arm. "Ann, wake up. You're snoring." The voice was unmistakably Mom's. At first, in that netherworld between sleep and consciousness, my sister accepted the notion that Mom was still alive. Nothing was more natural than her gentle hand upon Ann's arm and her reassuring voice prodding my sister into consciousness. Then the cobwebs dissipated from her brain and reality dictated the impossibility of the scenario. She was undoubtedly awake now - yet the hand remained on her arm. The presence remained in the room.

Slowly she turned her head without rolling over. In the darkened room she could see Mother's form kneeling at her bedside. The hand on her skin was solid and warm. Then fear overcame the moment! She wanted to turn over and face her but the experience was too overwhelming. "But you're dead!" she managed to utter. "You don't belong here. You're dead!"

Once again, the words were not audible but she had the feeling that Mom was saying, "but you asked me to come."

Ann lay perfectly still for a couple more minutes feeling the pressure of the hand on her arm and staring at her mother's solid form. Then the apparition slowly faded. The pressure faded from her arm. Alone in the room once more, she found the courage to sit up and turn on the bedside light. Through her tears, she reviewed the event in her mind. She hadn't dreamed the encounter. It was far too long in duration for that. Such a dream would have startled her into consciousness instantly. She lay back down and eventually fell asleep. When her alarm clock dragged her back to the physical world, her bedside light was still on - further confirmation of the reality of Mom's late-night visitation.

When Ann related these experiences to me, I asked her if she had mentioned them to anyone in her church congregation. She said that she hadn't. She was afraid of the negative response that she was sure to receive. I told her that she would be surprised to find out how many of these ordinary people had experienced extraordinary phenomena. Perhaps she took this as a challenge. Not long afterward she told me that she had related her experiences to a close friend of hers from her church, Cathy Rice (a pseudonym). Not only did Cathy readily accept Ann's story but had one of her own to relate in return.

Cathy's father had died in Tennessee, and she had gone down to attend the funeral. She remained in her mother's house for a couple of days thereafter to help her get through that trying period. Her father would sit in his rocking chair in the living room and exclaim, "Howdy," to anyone that would walk into the room. The presence of the old rocker was too much for her mother to handle at this time, so she had it removed to the laundry room.

On the day before Cathy was to return to Michigan, she was helping her mother by doing the laundry for her. When she walked into the room, her father's voice came loud and clear from the direction of the old rocker, "Howdy!"

"Dad, is that you?" Cathy shouted, after the initial shock had passed. There was no answer, yet she knew he was still there. "You're dead, Dad. You have to leave and go on." She waited a few minutes for a response. There was none. She hurriedly finished her task in the laundry room and left.

Like Ann, Cathy had been afraid to relate her experience to anyone out of fear of being called a liar or worse. Like many, (perhaps the reader included) it took someone else to come forward with a similar account before they felt comfortable in sharing their own.

The overwhelming consensus of the "down-to-earth" scientist, in instances like these, is that the experience is a fantasy born of grief. However, in the aforementioned book, "Hello From Heaven," there are several documented cases which disprove this theory.

One such account relates the story of a woman, whose fourteen-year-old daughter, Heather, was spending the night at her girlfriend's house. The woman and her husband had retired for the night at about 11:00 P.M. At 1:00 A.M. she was awakened by the telephone. A police dispatcher told her that the police were at her door and to please answer it. She got up and walked down the hallway toward the front door. She stopped short as she saw her father-in-law, who had died six years earlier, and her daughter, standing in midair in front of the door. Both were perfectly solid forms. They were both smiling at her as the grandfather had his arm around Heather. He said, "She's okay, Baby. I have her. She's fine!" Then the vision dissolved. When the woman was finally able to compose herself and answer the door, she was confronted by two uniformed police officers who's sad duty it was to inform her that her daughter had been killed in an automobile accident.

Obviously this woman was not grieving at the time of this incident. She had every reason to believe that her fourteen-year-old daughter was tucked safely in bed at that hour. Her father-in-law had been gone for six years. It would seem logical that she had accepted his passing by now. Yet, at a moment most apropos, a vision of the two of them presented itself to assure her that Heather was still alive and well and living in another dimension.

Another mainstream theory disproved by this case, (and many similar cases) is that of "residue haunting." The theory suggests that a person's energy pattern can imprint itself on its environment. According to this theory, a person's words and actions are recorded on inanimate objects in their immediate surroundings. In other words, the very walls of a home act as a tape recorder that records energy patterns and plays them back into the room indiscriminately. It has been my experience that, whenever I record something on a tape recorder, then play it back, it will play back exactly as it was originally recorded. In the aforementioned account, the grandfather had died when Heather was eight years old. How could the elderly man, during his earthly existence, have *ever* stood in the doorway (on the floor or in midair) with his arm around a fourteen-year-old Heather and said, "She's okay, Baby. I have her. She's fine!"?

Another theory is that our psychic subconscious perceives the information and projects it before our physical eyes like a hologram. Even if this were the case, (which it well might be in some situations), it is yet another example of the interconnectedness of the universal mind that may be tapped into at any given time, providing conditions are ripe.

A friend of a woman who had lost her little girl to leukemia was at a prayer meeting shortly after the girl's death. While in a meditative state, she saw a vision of little Suzie, who asked the woman to call her mother and to tell her "not to worry about my quilt."

She didn't feel right about calling the woman with such a message at that time. Again the vision of Suzie came to her and said, "Call my mother about the quilt." At this point, although she couldn't understand the meaning of this vision, she felt it was important that she do so. When she called, Suzie's mother said, "I'm so glad you called because yesterday was the worst day I've had since Suzie died. I was so upset that I got Suzie's quilt and went outside. I lay down under the tree and just cried and cried."

At this point she related the vision of Suzie and the message to "not worry about the quilt." She asked her if that meant anything to her. The mother began to cry and said, "you won't believe it, but when I was lying under the tree, crying, I was upset because Suzie had this quilt ever since she was a baby. She took it with her everywhere. She was never separated from it. When we buried her, I couldn't bear to part with her quilt. I felt so guilty about keeping it. You don't know how good it makes me feel to hear this. I'm so glad you called."

The woman receiving this otherworldly message had no idea about a quilt in connection with the deceased girl. Yet a vision of the girl had come to her to relay a message to her mother not to be upset with her decision not to include the quilt in her casket.

Was this incident an example of tapping into the universal consciousness or was Suzie reaching out from that other dimension to comfort her grieving mother? If the latter, why didn't she make her presence known to her mother directly instead of going through a friend? Perhaps the mother was not as receptive as the friend was. In either case, it was the mother that was grieving - not the friend.

"Hello From Heaven" also relates documented accounts of cases that involve more than one witness. Multiple-witness cases provide confirmation of the event and disprove both aforementioned theories. Confirmation was given in several of my own personal experiences:

The case of Lady and Uncle Harry

Smelling my grandmother's perfume at work.

The dog watching something unseen go from my wife to myself as a "cold spot" moved back and forth in concert with his eye movement.

And most notably, the seance in my sergeant's flat in Germany.

After reading this book, my sister has seemed to come to terms with the reality of these occasional visits from my mother. She has been able to incorporate this new information into her Christian belief system by rationalizing the fact that Jesus said, *"I will be with you always, even onto the end of the Earth."* (Matthew 28: 20) If Jesus is spirit and he is with us always, then why can't others in the spirit realm be with us too?

I, sadly, have not had the good fortune of seeing my mother since her death. Perhaps I too do not have the sensitivity to make contact with the nonphysical realm unless physical objects are directly affected. However, I am confident that when conditions are ripe and the opportunity presents itself, the veil between this dimension and the next will part and that unseen world will bleed through into this one for a brief time.

Chapter 10

Everyone there was crying and mourning for the child. Jesus said, "Don't cry; the child is not dead. She is only sleeping!" They all made fun of him, because they knew that she was dead. But Jesus took her by the hand and called out, "Get up, child!" Her life returned and she got up at once, and Jesus ordered them to give her something to eat. Her parents were astounded, but Jesus commanded them not to tell anyone what had happened. (Luke 8: 52 56)

Jesus said this and then added, "Our friend Lazarus has fallen asleep, but I will go and wake him up." The disciples answered, "If he is asleep, Lord, he will get well." Jesus meant that Lazarus had died, but they thought he meant natural sleep, so Jesus told them plainly, "Lazarus is dead, but for your sake I am glad that I was not with him, so that you will believe. Let us go to him." (John 11: 11 - 15)

Martha, the dead man's sister, answered, "There will be a bad smell, Lord. He has been buried four days!" (John 11: 39)

After he had said this, he called out in a loud voice, "Lazarus, come out! He came out, his hands and feet wrapped in grave cloths, and with a cloth around his face. "Untie him," Jesus told them, "and let him go." (John 11: 43 - 44)

Forty years ago, a common joke was; "No one knows what the afterlife is really like. No one has ever died and come back to tell us about it." Today, with the advancement of resuscitation techniques, the aforementioned statement no longer applies. With the overwhelming volume of case studies from around the world, few people are unaware of the common factors involved pertaining to NDE's (near death experiences).

As a rule, all goes black for the subject, then they can see everything around them in the physical world. Invariably they will find themselves floating in the air and looking back down at their lifeless physical form. If there are doctors and nurses working on their body, they are able to see them and hear their conversation. They find themselves indifferent to the revelation that they have died. At this point, they will find themselves hurling through a dark tunnel with a pinpoint of light at the end. The light gradually grows larger as they approach it. Their only desire is to reach that brilliant, warm light that generates unconditional love.

When they reach the light, they are enveloped by it. The properties of it are such that the subject finds it impossible to describe in conventional terms. They say that the light is so bright that if they were to view it with their physical eyes, they would surely be blinded. They find that it is not simply a light but a "being of light" that greets them.

At this point, they are presented with a "life review." Everything they had done, said, thought, felt or witnessed in the life they had just left is shown to them in detail. Some say that it is like a motion picture projected on a screen. Others claim to actually relive every moment of their past life. Every detail, no matter how seemingly insignificant, is presented for scrutiny. The "light being" is not in the least judgmental of the subject. It simply asks, "What have you done with your life to show me?" The subject is then allowed to judge their own spiritual growth.

It is usually at this point that they are reunited with loved ones that have gone over to the other side of life before them. These souls are not judgmental either. They, like the light being, exude total, unconditional love and acceptance.

Often a subject's otherworldly journey will be more extensive. However, the aforementioned process is common to most NDE's. It is usually at this point that the subject is given the choice to stay in this spiritual realm or return to their physical body to complete unfinished business. Most subjects balk at the idea of leaving this celestial realm of beauty, peace and love. Often they are told that they must return. However, most of them realize on their own the importance of their mission in the physical plane and, after some convincing, voluntarily return to a corporal encasement that is usually wracked with pain. Almost always, before their return, they are left with one final message from the spirit realm . . . "The key to life is love."

After this experience, the NDE subject's life tends to change dramatically. They are no longer afraid of that transformation known as death. They have no desire to take their own life, as they understand the importance of it, yet they await that time of metamorphosing with a keen sense of longing for that state of existence of peace and awareness.

Quite often one who has had an NDE will develop psychic skills that were not present before their experience. Clairvoyance, precognition, telepathy, psychokinesis, automatic writing as well as healing others by the laying on of hands are just some of the talents inherited by an NDE. Often an NDE patient will affect metallic objects or electrical devices by their mere proximity. Not only do NDE patients make claim to these abilities but are able to demonstrate them to the amazement of mainstream scientists under rigid laboratory conditions.

(Note: Many of the same psychic abilities are present in alien abductees.)

Several books and articles have been written on the subject of the near death experience. The so-called "father" of the NDE is Raymond A. Moody, Jr., M.D. After many years of dealing with death and dying, Dr. Moody had compiled several cases where patients, who had clinically died and were resuscitated, reported virtually identical experiences. In 1975, Dr. Moody published his first book on the subject, "Life After Life," in which many of these cases were related. His book commanded the attention of Dr. Elisabeth Kubler-Ross who, unbeknownst to Moody, was conducting similar research. When the two doctors got together and compared notes, they found that their findings were duplicated.

Dr. Moody's public airing of NDEs brought a flood of reports from patients who had, heretofore, remained silent about their experience out of fear of ridicule or suspicion of insanity. Moody followed his first with other books containing more such cases. After that, other physicians, psychologists and NDE patients began to fill the bookshelves with similar accounts. Dr. Moody had opened the floodgates to the scientific community that proved beyond a reasonable doubt that the near death experience is a universal phenomenon.

Immediately the hard-core skeptics, in a vain attempt to hold on to established dogma, set out to assign a prosaic explanation to the NDE phenomenon. They reasoned that the "imagery" of hurling through a tunnel toward a bright light was merely a re-enactment of the birth process. Any woman who has given birth can attest to the fact (much to their chagrin) that the baby does not "hurl" through the birth canal. It is a much-too-slow and arduous process.

They argue that the brain of a dying person produces a natural opium called endorphin. This endorphin may induce hallucinations in the patient to ease the shock of the fact that their life is ending. Morphine, Demerol or like drugs are often administered to a dying patient. These drugs could cause the same effect. The misfiring of a million neurons in the center of the brain could account for the tunnel of light effect.

Then there is the old "frontal lobe" excuse. Under clinically controlled conditions, doctors have tested volunteer subjects who are seated in a comfortable chair with a special helmet placed on their head. The helmet is rigged with electrodes. They are left alone in a cubicle while the doctor controls the electrodes from an observation room. Different areas of the subject's brain are systematically stimulated. It has been found that when the frontal lobe is stimulated, the subject will experience a light-headed feeling. Sometimes they will feel that they are floating or literally out of their bodies. Some have reported sensing a presence in the room with them.

This experiment has also been used to explain the alien abduction experience. However, like the alien abduction experience, it falls short of explaining all the other elements of the phenomenon.

It has been argued that this being of light encountered by the patient is the result of their Christian conditioning. They do not take into account the fact that this light being is encountered by Christians, Muslims, Hindus, Buddhists, Jews, Satanists and atheists alike.

These conventional explanations do not address the fact that children as young as three (before their minds can be indoctrinated with their parents' ideologies) report the same experiences. In many cases these small children describe family members that they had met on the other side. They are able to identify them by name and relay messages from these deceased loved ones. Only afterwards is it established that the family member had died before the child's birth. The child had never seen a picture of the person in question. Nor could the child have any knowledge of the subject matter to which the message referred.

Another element of an NDE, not explained by conventional wisdom, is that often the patient will report to doctors what was being said and done in the operating theater while he or she was clinically dead. Often they will relate complicated medical procedures that were performed on their bodies, as they watched while hovering near the ceiling. On occasion the patient can relate, with astonishing accuracy, what was being said and done by family members in the waiting room. Geographical location presents no restriction, as the patient will later inform friends or family members, who are hundreds of miles away, what they were wearing, saying and doing at the exact time of their "death."

Ex-drug users, who have had an NDE, have stated that they know the difference between their experience and a drug-induced hallucination. Even dyed-in-the-wool scientists are forced to change their opinion after personally witnessing the "tunnel of light."

When all else fails, the down-to-earth scientist will simply state that the NDE phenomenon is just "a new cultural myth." It is clear, however, that, albeit to a lesser degree, out-of-body experiences have been recorded throughout history. Folklore from all corners of the planet relates identical experiences. The Bible also has its fair share of such claims. Is it possible that myths, folklore and Bible stories have a basis in fact?

I was sixteen years old when I was graciously allowed to join a group called "The Dearborn Hypnotist and Mental Research Association." A very official sounding title for a handful of middle-aged and elderly gentlemen who considered themselves freelance hypnotists and investigators of metaphysical matters. Our meeting place would rotate between each member's home monthly. The host would supply the coffee and doughnuts and, for two hours preceding refreshment time, we would discuss the more socially unacceptable aspects of world reality.

One evening, a member related his first encounter with OBEs (out-of-body experiences) to the group. He was lying on the bank of a river. The setting was peaceful and serene. One moment he was consciously enjoying his surroundings. The next moment he was asleep. The next moment he was again conscious, standing and looking down at his body, resting peacefully on the ground. He was amazed at his predicament and wondered if he had died. Yet he recalls gazing down at the empty shell that was his physical form, only moments before, with curious indifference.

He decided to take a stroll along the river bank. There was no one to be seen. The setting was exactly as it was before he had drifted off to sleep. One would think that if this were a dream, other characters would come into play. One would also think that the dreamer would not question his situation - not realize that he was disembodied - and certainly not remain conscious without awakening in the physical body. Yet remain conscious he did for several minutes, as he strolled along the river bank and drank in the beauty of his surroundings in more vibrant detail than he had ever witnessed.

He did not recall returning to his body. All of a sudden he was awake and in physical form. The experience was so dramatic that it had left a lasting impression on his mind. He also was determined to prove or disprove the feasibility of this phenomenon. His investigations harvested volumes of documentation that introduced him to OBEs.

My sixteen-year-old brain began working overtime. Is it possible to leave one's body and return unscathed? I had never heard of OBEs before and had never given the possibility of it as much as a passing thought. Now I was exhilarated by the very idea of it!

Though amateurs, most of the group's members were trained and well-seasoned hypnotists. Within the few months that I had been a member, they had taken me under their wing and taught me the art of self-hypnosis. I had practiced this new found art nightly. I found that I could set my mind like an alarm clock. If I knew the exact time upon retiring for the evening, I could hypnotize myself, with a post-hypnotic suggestion to awaken at a given time, and awaken exactly at that time. Hitherto, this technique was good for little more. Now I had another purpose for it. Another challenge! And (being sixteen and invincible) damn the consequences!

I knew that my father's alarm clock would sound precisely at 4:30 A.M. I would not want him to come in to check on me and find me "dead." I had to include a return to my body by that time. I lay in bed, took note of the time and, picking the usual spot on the ceiling to concentrate on, began my relaxation exercise. I told myself that I would fall into a natural sleep and leave my body, becoming conscious only after I had done so. I carefully added that I would return to the physical body by 4:30 A.M. I gave myself the final command of, "sleep, Dave" and felt myself drifting down. Within five minutes I lost consciousness.

My next conscious memory was bobbing on the ceiling like a buoy on water and looking down at my physical counterpart sleeping peacefully. It had worked! I didn't know how but it had and . . . now what should I do? Anything I wanted, I supposed. I was "out" and free!

It was the week between Christmas and New Years, 1964. I had just been let go from my first job as stock boy at a five and dime where I had been hired as part-time Christmas help. I could go there! No sooner had the thought entered my head than I was on my way. Trees, houses, streetlights rushed past me en route. It was as if I were standing still and the landscape was whizzing past me in a blur. When the rush stopped, I was standing in front of the store. The doors were locked and the security lights were the only thing that illuminated the store's interior. I thought, "How will I get in?" And I was inside. Oversized white sheets had been draped over the merchandise counters, as was the practice upon closing for the night. Had it been a dream, I would expect to see customers roaming the aisles, the merchandise exposed, the overhead fluorescent lights brightly lit and my boss assigning my next chore before I had completed the one I was doing. This was not the case. Things were exactly as they should be in the wee hours of the morning at the five and dime.

I walked down an aisle to my left and to the back of the store. I entered the doorway to the break room. Everything was as it should be, although there was no one there but me. A kitchen table in the middle of the room had been cleaned of debris, save one large ashtray in the center, and the coffeepot was empty and set up for the morning. I made a mental note of these facts and moved on through the room and out the other side.

Walking up the aisle on the other side of the store toward the front, I realized that I had not kept track of time. " I must be back in my body by 4:30," and that thought caused another rush of landscape - this time much faster. I found myself in our kitchen, leaning against the sink.

I don't recall looking at the clock but I was aware of the fact that it was still early morning and everyone was still asleep. I walked into the living room and sat on the couch. I looked at the Christmas tree. Of course it was unplugged and there were no lamps lit in the house, yet the room seemed to be fairly bright with a light from a source that was impossible to identify.

I have no idea how long I sat there pondering my situation. Then I heard my father's alarm clock ring. I was still out of my body! For a split second I panicked. There was a loud "pop" in both ears and my physical body jerked. I lay in bed trying to move. I was paralyzed! I was horrified! Was this a consequence of the OBE? Would my few hours of freedom, to travel to a closed dime store in my spirit body, cost me the use of the physical one for the rest of my life? I heard my father get up and head for the bathroom. I decided not to fight the paralysis. I lay still and, a few seconds later, feeling returned to my entire body at once. I moved every part of my body I could think of, just to make sure that I could.

I continued to lie there with mixed emotions. What a wonderful and frightening revelation! What the old man had told me was true. We exist and are aware independent of our physical bodies!

I couldn't get word of my instant success to the group fast enough. When I did, I was warned of the dangers involved in the practice. I was told that another spirit could possess my body while I was out. That the more I projected, the more I would want to do so until it became an obsession. That the astral or silver cord, which connects the physical body to the spirit body, could break and I would never be able to return.

Mr. West, the man who had taught me self-hypnosis, gave me his copy of a book entitled, "The Projection of the Astral Body," by Sylvan Muldoon and Hereward Carrington. It was first published in London in 1929. In 1964 it was out of print but was re-released in 1973 in paperback form. (Fortunately for me, as a friend's dog made a meal of the copy I had been given.) The information contained between its covers proved priceless in my quest for the truth regarding not only astral projection but the continuance of conscious existence after death.

Sylvan Muldoon and his sister had experienced spontaneous astral projection since they were small children. Sometimes they would meet and play together in the early morning hours outside their home . . . in their spirit bodies. As Muldoon got older, he was shocked to find out the uniqueness of their abilities. He and his sister thought that leaving the body at night was the normal procedure for everyone.

As a teenager he began experimenting with the process. He found that one could travel in spirit to any distant point - to the far reaches of the universe - and return as a function of the astral cord. The cord acts as an umbilical cord that connects the physical and astral counterparts. The body is the machine and the spirit is the "battery" that supplies the energy that animates it. When the battery is run down, the body requires sleep so the astral body may move slightly out of coincidence from the physical to be recharged with cosmic energy. Often a dream or mere thought, on the part of the sleeper, will cause the astral body to project further away from the physical body, resulting in astral travel.

When the spirit is within approximately ten feet of the physical, the cord is about two inches in diameter. As the spirit moves further away, its diameter decreases to about an eighth of an inch and remains at that size indefinitely. Regardless of the diameter of the cord or the expanse between the two counterparts, the same life-sustaining spark will continue to supply the physical body with enough energy to keep it functional (albeit in suspended animation).

I was surprised and relieved to learn that many aspects of *my* OBE were exactly what I should expect to experience. As a rule, one always looks back at the sleeping body. A desire to travel to any geographical destination will speed them on their way. Travel in the astral body can be at four different speeds:

- A normal walk.
- Fast motion
- Super fast motion
- Instantaneous

According to Muldoon, when one is in motion, it will appear to the subject that they are standing still and the landscape is moving past them. Even though spirit can pass through solid objects, they are able to walk across the floor or sit on furniture. They are used to doing so in the physical, thus their thought sustains them. Should they question their ability to do so for a moment, they would drop straight through the object. He also explains that when the spirit (wherein lies the seat of consciousness) is startled or excited or the physical body is abruptly disturbed, the astral counterpart will immediately withdraw into the physical. When it slams back into the body, the shock causes temporary paralysis.

His experimentation, while projected, yielded evidence that while the astral body is within ten feet of the physical, the magnetic pull between the two causes the astral body to be unstable. It will bounce up and down, to and fro, until it has moved far enough away from the physical that the astral cord is thinner. At this point it will stabilize.

I found evidence of this fact during a spontaneous projection while napping, one late afternoon, years later. I had returned home from work about 4:30 P.M. and, being quite exhausted, flopped, face down on the bed to rest. It was my wife's practice, after making the bed, to adorn it with several stuffed animals. Perhaps she was in a rush that day because, though the bed had been made, it was devoid of her fluffy wildlife.

It took little time for me to fall asleep. Almost instantly I was standing at the foot of the bed, semiconscious, looking at my body. Everything in the room was bouncing up and down. I looked to my left and saw my wife's big stuffed teddy bear, Fred, sitting on the floor. It was alive to me, in my half-dream state, as it was jumping up and down. I watched the bed with my body on it bouncing. I didn't want to move for fear of being jostled off my feet but I gathered the courage and went to the side of the bed. I knelt down and looked under the bed to see two other stuffed animals on the floor to the far side of the bed. I reasoned that these two were responsible for the disturbance. They must be the ones shaking the bed.

I stood up and looked through the bedroom door to see the bathroom door down the hall. Though everything was still bouncing, I decided to move toward the hallway. As soon as I moved out of the bedroom, everything stopped bouncing and I became completely conscious. "My God," I thought, "am I dead?" With that thought, the hallway disappeared and another door was directly in front of me. All was dark around me but the room in front of me was brightly lit. The door was wide open and I could see white walls with a lone crucifix mounted at eye level. I stood frozen for several seconds. An unseen force prohibited me from advancing.

From my left, within the room, a young man, who looked familiar but I could not place, stepped to the open door. He looked out at me and gently but firmly said, "we're not ready for you yet." I made no reply. I took one last look at that enticing enclosure beyond the open door and retreated.

I awakened in the same position in which I had fallen asleep. I got up and frantically tried to make sense of my "dream." Standing at the foot of the bed, I looked to my left. There sat Fred, staring up at me with big, black button eyes. I hadn't recalled taking notice of his position when entering the room but perhaps my subconscious registered it. I did know that the floor was not his usual resting place. I also knew that I did not look under the bed before lying down. I went to the side of the bed as I had in my dream, knelt down and looked underneath. There, lying on the floor at the far side of the bed, were the same two stuffed animals in the same position that I had perceived them minutes before while projected.

Did my query as to my death instantly catapult me to that door that separates this dimension from the next? Was that door the same one referred to by Steve's father in a previous chapter? ("I have to go now. Steve is waiting for me at the door.") Had I walked through that door, would I be writing these words now or would I have been unable to return to the physical? At what point does the projection of the astral body become permanent?

Before the silver cord is loosed, or the golden bowl is broken, or the pitcher is broken at the fountain, or the wheel broken at the cistern, and the dust returneth to the earth as it was, and the spirit returneth unto God who gave it. (Ecclesiastes 12: 6 - 7)

Here, the Bible clearly states that when the silver cord is "loosed" or severed and the "golden bowl" or vessel for the spirit (physical body) is broken, then shall the body's clay composition revert back to its original elements and the soul return to that universal consciousness we refer to as God.

This brings us full-circle to the passages mentioned at the beginning of this chapter. In both instances, of Lazarus and the little girl, Jesus told those gathered around that they were not dead - only sleeping. In both cases, he recalled the spirit and the spirit returned to animate the body. In the case of the little girl, Jesus was right outside the house when word came that she had died. He would have been able to resuscitate her before irreversible damage occurred to the brain and other vital organs. As to Lazarus, however, he had been "dead" and entombed for four days. Martha, Lazarus' sister, was correct in assuming that there would be a great stench as rigor mortis would have, long since, set in. Lazarus' tomb in Bethany, would have acted as an oven in the searing heat of the desert Sun, hastening the decay of the muscles and organs, rendering them useless. His brain would have atrophied, reducing it to a vegetative state, even if it were possible to resume blood flow through it.

Some medical conditions display symptoms that mimic death. The practice of embalming became law, in the early 1900s, after it was discovered that many people, thought to be dead, were buried alive.

It has been demonstrated that a body, in a state of suspended animation, can survive for days without food, water and very little air. It can also withstand extreme cold or heat without adverse effects once the body has been restored to normalcy. As long as the silver or astral cord remains connected to the physical, enough life-giving support is given to the body to sustain it.

Jesus, being a highly advanced spiritual entity, was able to see both on the physical and spiritual planes. He could see, in these situations, that the cord was still attached. He could communicate with their spirit and retrieve it to the physical counterpart. There were other instances where loved ones had died and Jesus could do little more than to give those who survived them loving assurance of the wonderful place where they had gone. What made these cases different? Jesus told us. *"They are not dead. They are sleeping."*

Those around Him chided Him for His analysis of the situation. But instead of offering a detailed and probably unacceptable explanation, He simply recalled their spirit and proved His point.

This is not to undermine the abilities that Jesus possessed and displayed. To recall a spirit to its body, before the silver cord is severed and death is imminent, is a feat worthy of only the most highly advanced spiritual entity. It is only to say that, in light of the volume of evidence that has been garnered concerning NDEs and OBEs, (not to mention what Jesus Himself has taught regarding the human soul) this theory is the more practical.

Is it, then, that the soul springs into existence at conception or birth, then detaches itself from the physical at death and joins the universal consciousness for eternity? Such a theory would contradict the very definition of the word "eternity." Eternity not only means "without an end," it also means "without a beginning." A continuous and uninterrupted cycle of existence. Has something been overlooked in western orthodoxies that present seeming contradictions? Or has something been purposefully expunged?

Chapter 11

Then the disciples asked Jesus, "Why do the teachers of the law say that Elijah has to come first?" "Elijah is indeed coming first," answered Jesus, "and he will get everything ready. But I tell you that Elijah has already come and people did not recognize him, but treated him just as they pleased. In the same way they will also mistreat the son of man." Then the disciples understood that he was talking to them about John the Baptist.
(Matthew 17: 10 - 13)

    At first blush, this passage would seem to indicate that Jesus was saying to His disciples that the spirit of John the Baptist was previously incarnated as Elijah. How could the Christian Bible, which denounces the concept of the transmigration of souls (reincarnation), contain a passage with such a connotation? When one considers historic fact and the early teachings of Jesus and His disciples, the answer becomes obvious. Oversight!
    Western theologies teach that the spirit must endure but one lifetime in the flesh. Reincarnation is an Eastern theory and is not accepted or tolerated by Christians. However, it is historically true that Jesus (being from the East) preached reincarnation as gospel. Origen De Principiis (185 - 254 A.D.), whom the Encyclopedia Britannica referred to as "the most prominent of the church fathers with the possible exception of Saint Augustine," devoted his life to spreading the gospel of Jesus. The transmigration of souls was a large part of his teachings. He was quoted as saying:
    "Every soul comes into this world strengthened by the victories or weakened by the defeats of its previous life. Its place in this world as a vessel appointed to honor or dishonor, is determined by its previous merits or demerits. Its work in this world determines its place in the world which is to follow this."
    Other early church fathers, who were revered as Saints and are to this day, echoed the same message:
    "We were in being long before the foundation of the world;

We existed in the eye of God, for it is our destiny to live in Him. We are reasonable creatures of the Divine Word; Therefore, we have existed from the beginning, for in the beginning was the word." (St. Clement of Alexandria. 150 - 220 A.D.)

"It is absolutely necessary that the soul should be healed and purified. If this does not take place during its life on Earth, it must be accomplished in future lives." (St. Gregory. 257 - 332 A.D.)

"The message of Plato, the purest and the most luminous of all philosophy, has at last scattered the darkness of error, and now shines forth mainly in Plotinus, a Platonist so like his master that one would think they lived together, or rather, since so long a period of time separates them, that Plato was born again in Plotinus." (St. Augustine. 354 - 430 A.D.)

"Know that if you become worse you will go to the worse souls, and if better, to the better souls. And in every succession of life and death you will suffer what like must fitly suffer at the hands of like." (The Republic. Plato. 582 - 507 B.C.)

Plato's words are paraphrased by Paul, while teaching Jesus' gospel. *"For whatever a man soweth, that will he also reap."* (Galatians 6: 7)

In tracing the Bible's history, we find that the scriptures existed in their entirety before the fourth century A.D. In A.D. 325, Constantine, the Emperor of Rome, appointed Damascus as pope of the Catholic church. Between these two, they founded the Council of Nicaea. It was advantageous, if not imperative at that time, to have the Emperor on the side of the church. But there was a price to pay for this cooperative. Constantine would dictate the content of what would become the last word on Christian orthodoxy. The scriptures were gathered and carefully sifted through to make certain that any and all references to reincarnation were purged from its content.

The Emperor felt that his subjects would feel that if they did not live a perfect life this time they could always make up for it in the next. The church agreed with this assessment. Thus, the church/government could better control the masses through fear. Still, the traditional teachings of Jesus on the matter were passed on. Zealot followers of the living Christ stubbornly refused to forsake His gospel simply because a newly founded allegiance between church and state omitted the words from "The Book."

Then, in the fifth century A.D., Emperor Justinian formed the fifth Ecumenical Council which assembled in Constantinople.

The sole purpose of this council was to permanently squelch, once and for all, the reincarnation dogma. Justinian had his own reasons for wishing to believe in the one-life doctrine. Like most Roman Emperors, he was a tyrant responsible for the wrongful deaths of many innocent people. He could not abide the thought of having to return to flesh for the purpose of atoning for his misdeeds. So, like an ostrich with its head in the sand, he reasoned that if the doctrine was not in print and the church's followers abandoned the belief, it would not exist. This accomplished, he could then "live by the sword" without having to "die by the sword."

From that time forward, Christians who included reincarnation in their belief system were persecuted and put to death. This reign of terror persisted not only by the government but by the church until the thirteenth century when the last vestiges of reincarnation had been wiped out. And yet, with all the careful deletions from scripture on the matter of reincarnation, some passages, such as the one above, that hint at the phenomenon, were overlooked.

The concept of reincarnation states that every soul was in existence since the beginning. Like an electrical spark in our own physical brains, each individual soul is a spark from that universal consciousness. Souls began inhabiting physical organisms as a matter of exploration and expression. They soon became entangled in the trappings of the physical experience and lost sight of their prime objective - to learn the lessons of life, advance spiritually and again become one with their Creator.

There is the law of "karma" and the law of "grace." The law of karma states, "whatever wrong one might commit against another must be meted out to that individual in like kind." *"An eye for an eye. A tooth for a tooth."* "If you live by the sword, you must die by the sword." "As you sow, so shall you reap." The golden rule (*do unto others as you would have them do unto you*) is just another way of saying, "*as you do unto others, so shall it be done unto you.*"

What weight does this rule carry if one "lives by the sword" and dies a natural death? If a person murders another and is never caught, punished or put to death, this edict would certainly lose its clout under the one-life doctrine. However, the law of karma provides that, if one person takes the life of another, both souls must return to flesh in a future lifetime to right that wrong. This time, of course, the murderer would become the murdered and vice-versa. The child-abuser would become the abused child. The rapist would become the rape victim and so on. How many times have you asked yourself why God would allow such injustices in the world? Why a child must be the victim of physical or sexual abuse? Why a person must die so young? Why do bad things happen to good people? Perhaps it's not a matter of God *allowing* these things to happen at all. Perhaps it is a matter of *us* exercising our God-given gift of free will - and paying the karmic debt along the way.

But if this is true, two souls would have to return for the sole purpose of satisfying their karmic debt to the other. Even if this were accomplished, what further karmic debt would both parties accumulate to others in that lifetime? Now they must return again and again until they have paid their debt without creating new ones. It would become a vicious cycle. How could that cycle be broken without the individual attaining perfection? Enter, then, the law of grace.

The law of grace, simply put, is remorse and forgiveness. If the offender can show heartfelt remorse for their actions and the aggrieved can truly forgive the offence, then the matter is dropped and the debt may go unpaid. More eloquently put; *"Forgive us our debts, as we forgive our debtors."* (Matthew 6: 12)

If life is eternal, then where is the equity in giving a soul one short earthly lifetime to prove its worth to a merciful, loving Father? If a thousand years is but a day in the eyes of God and a man lived one hundred years, his earthly life would be one tenth of a day to God. It would be like us saying to our own child at birth, "you must learn right from wrong, pay for any and all mistakes that you might make and prove yourself worthy of the Kingdom of Heaven. Now, I'm going to give you exactly two hours and twenty-four minutes in which to do it. So you'd better get started!"

Proponents of the reincarnation theory, as well as near death patients, agree that each consecutive physical experience is likened to a school term. One learns what lessons that class has to offer or they must repeat the class. Once they have learned these lessons, they move onto the next grade. There are many lessons to learn and a soul must experience everything before it may graduate. That graduation occurs only when the soul has reached perfection. It is at that point that it reunites with the universal consciousness (God). Hell, on the other hand, is total separation from God. It is not a "lake of fire and brimstone in the center of the earth." This interpretation is a man-made image that was projected to the masses, once again, to gain control through fear. The purpose for this frightening image works almost as well today as it did hundreds of years ago. However, the myth of the torments of hell is beginning to lose its desired effect, as mankind learns more and more about his physical and spiritual environment.

In the 1960's Dr. Ian Stevenson, M.D., a psychiatrist at the University of Virginia Medical College, became world-renowned after publishing his findings on the study of reincarnation. His book "Twenty Cases Suggestive of Reincarnation" represented twenty cases out of the six hundred he had thoroughly investigated. The cases he had selected to relate in this volume left little room for debate as to their authenticity or lack of a prosaic explanation.

One case was that of a little boy in India who, from the age of three, told his parents that he was not who they thought he was at all. He related details of his former life such as his name, addresses, the city in India where he had lived, the names of family members, where he had worked, how old he was when he died and the fact that he was murdered by a thief in a robbery attempt. A large black birthmark on the boy's forehead was reported to be where he had been shot and killed as a young man in his previous incarnation. The town in which the boy claimed to have lived was several miles from the village where the boy was born. Neither he nor his family had been out of their village since the boy's birth. The boy was about six years old when Dr. Stevenson investigated the case. Stevenson garnered as much information as possible from the boy, his family and the people of the village that knew about the young man's wild assertions. Then, accompanied by Stevenson and his investigative team, the family journeyed to the town in question in an effort to verify the details given by the boy.

Before they even arrived, the boy was able to predict landmarks and roads in and out of town as though he had made the trip a thousand times. Once there, he guided the entourage to where he had lived in his previous life. The boy was overjoyed to be reunited with his "old family." Though the family members were at first skeptical, they were soon convinced when the boy told them things that only the deceased man could have known. While walking through the main street of town, the boy walked up to a perfect stranger and insisted that he owed him money and named the amount. After the purpose of their sojourn was explained to the man, he told them that he had indeed owed that sum of money - but not to the boy - to the man that the boy claimed to have been before his death.

Though Dr. Stevenson had accumulated many such case histories, he was careful to include in his writings only accounts that had been professionally investigated and whose validity was beyond reproach. His meticulous approach to detail was rewarded when the Journal of the American Medical Association declared, "In regard to reincarnation, he (Stevenson) has painstakingly and unemotionally collected a detailed series of cases from India. Cases in which the evidence is difficult to explain on any other grounds."

Stevenson realized that extraordinary claims required extraordinary proof. As evidenced in the 1950's, when Morey Bernstein, a prominent psychiatrist and hypnotist, went out on a limb with his book, "The Search for Bridey Murphy." While hypnotizing a patient, Jean Simmons, he unwittingly regressed her to a life before her birth as Bridey Murphy. Bernstein, though startled by this twist in the session, pursued the matter more deeply, gathering as much information about this alleged personality as possible. Jean Simmons, while under hypnosis, related a life as the wife of a barrister in Ireland in the 1800s. It was, by most standards, an average lifetime with no particularly outstanding achievements that might have earned "Bridey" an article in the history books. (It is interesting to note here that few people who recall past lives, either consciously or while under hypnosis, claim to be a Napoleon, Hitler, Longfellow or Jesus Christ. Most purport to have been members of the commonwealth, living varied lives - dying varied deaths. Many give details that can be vouched for only through public records and descendants.)

After the book was published, the skeptics had a field day. They investigated Jean Simmons, digging deep into her past (present life, that is) trying to expose her as a fraud or at least offer a scientific explanation. They discovered that, when Simmons was a child, she had an Irish nanny. It was reasoned that the nanny had told the young girl stories of her own life in Ireland and these same stories were rising to the surface from Jean's subconscious.

Bernstein suffered a great deal of ridicule from the scientific community and the public at large for nine years. However, all he was guilty of was not doing his homework before releasing the book. In 1965, William J. Barker, after eliminating the nanny as a possible explanation and digging into public records in Ireland, published his findings in "The Search for Bridey Murphy With New Material." He had discovered that a Bridey Murphy did indeed exist in the time frame that Jean Simmons had reported. Names, dates, addresses and pertinent facts about the late Murphy coincided with uncanny accuracy to Jean Simmons' testimony while under hypnosis.

Raymond Moody (discussed in the previous chapter) wrote about *his* past nine lives, discovered while undergoing a past-life-regression, in "Coming Back: A Psychiatrist Explores Past-Life Journeys."

Brian L. Weiss treated the subject in "Many Lives, Many Masters."

The world-renowned Edgar Cayce, better known as "the sleeping prophet," spoke often of the transmigration of souls while in trance. After his death, all of the 14,000 transcripts of his trance sessions, were released in book and CD form. Although one book dealt exclusively with the subject, all of them contained references to the fact that we must return to physical form until perfection is achieved.

Cayce (1877 - 1945) was born and reared as an orthodox Christian in Kentucky. He prided himself on the fact that he had read the Bible from cover to cover once for every year of his life. He first discovered his psychic gift as a child when, unable to retain what he had read in his school books, he fell asleep using a book as a pillow. Upon awakening, he found that he could recite any paragraph on any page of that book, verbatim, that one could quiz him on.

At the age of twenty-one, he developed paralysis of the throat that threatened to completely destroy his voice. When the doctors could do nothing more for him, out of desperation, he experimented with the same method he had used for the purpose of learning. This time, when he put himself into a trance state, another entity spoke through him. The voice was not that of

Cayce's. The articulate dialog and verbiage was far from that of the waking Cayce. This "spirit guide" claimed to know much about the spiritual and physical realms and spoke often and reverently of Jesus and His teachings. The entity diagnosed Cayce's problem and recommended a specific treatment consisting mostly of natural herbs. Cayce followed the directions to the letter and soon overcame the paralysis - much to the surprise of his physicians.

His wife and secretary began experimenting with the entranced Cayce to see if he could locate an individual and identify any physical malady they might possess. They were immediately successful in doing so. As before, the entity, through Cayce, would give specific directions for the subject to follow that would relieve or completely eradicate the condition. If the subject would follow the instructions, the success rate far exceeded the odds of chance.

Cayce was never consciously aware of what was coming through him while in a trance state. He could only rely upon the transcripts meticulously recorded by his secretary. One day, after an exhaustive trance session, he was appalled to learn that information that had just come through him indicated the cause of the physical problems of the subject, for which the reading was intended, stemmed from a previous life. The very implication of reincarnation was blasphemous in light of his Christian upbringing. Cayce reasoned that this must be the work of the devil and vowed never to repeat the process as long as he lived.

He was good to his word until his own son took ill and, once again, the doctors could do nothing to save him. Cayce then broke his vow and had his secretary write the transcript of yet another life saving reading. In the years to follow, many seemingly incurable physical maladies were put in check as a result of Cayce's trance sessions. Furthermore, he came to accept the concept of reincarnation and assimilate it into his western orthodox belief system.

In "Edgar Cayce's Story of Jesus," edited by Jeffrey Furst, the bombshell is dropped on the first page of the first chapter. The entranced Cayce is asked when Jesus first realized that He would be the Savior of the world. The answer given was, "When He fell in Eden." The implication that the spirit of Jesus of Nazareth originally occupied the body of the first man (Adam) is a bit farfetched for any Christian to accept. However, further readings lend credence to this statement.

Jesus said that every man must pay for his own sin, not the sins of his father or anyone else, and must do so "in this life." Once again, how is this possible if a man lives by the sword and dies a natural death? Unless a future incarnation is considered to be "in this life" (or within this physical realm). Who was it that shed his blood and gave his life for the atonement of the sins of all mankind? Jesus! Who was it that plunged the world of man into sin and death because of his *own* original sin? Adam! If this edict, given by Jesus, is a hard and fast universal law, who would be the most likely candidate to give his life for the remission of the original sin? Adam!

The readings go on to say that the spiritual entity, which was once Adam, also came back as Enoch, Melchizedek, Joseph, Joshua, Jeshua, then as Jesus. Although at one point in the readings, it was mentioned that the same entity reincarnated thirty times before inhabiting the body of Jesus. After the lifetime of Jesus, perfection was accomplished, the karmic debt had been paid and the soul, mostly known as Jesus the Christ of Nazareth, at long last, returned to be one with the living God.

In John 8: 56 - 58, Jesus' own words alluded to this fact. *"Your father Abraham rejoiced that he was to see the time of my coming. He saw it and was glad."* They said to him, *"you are not even fifty years old - and you have seen Abraham?"* *"I am telling you the truth,"* Jesus replied, *"Before Abraham was born, 'I Am'."*

Then there is the ever controversial phrase, *"I am telling you the truth: No one can see the Kingdom of God without being born again."* (John 3: 3) Some interpret this to mean one is "born again" when they accept Jesus as their Savior. Baptists interpret it as the act of baptism. To be born again of spirit could also refer to physical death, when the "silver cord" or "ethereal umbilical cord" is severed. But in light of Jesus' original teachings, that have been shown to be historically true, the overlooked passages in the Bible that allude to reincarnation, and the volume of scientifically controlled evidence supporting the theory, perhaps Jesus' words should be taken at face value.

The "sleeping prophet" also stated that, "the Earth is but an atom in a universe of worlds." If a soul is required to animate the physical body of humankind, it would necessarily follow that one would be required of any intelligent being inhabiting any celestial body in the universe. (Actually *any* living creature - but that is not up to debate in this volume.) Furthermore, if there is but one God of the universe, He would be *their* God as well as ours. If the original teachings of Jesus are true and reincarnation is a fact, there can be no restrictions as to the planet on which a soul might choose to incarnate. We (humans and aliens alike) would all be considered as one brotherhood of souls under the auspices of the same God.

Is this the message that the "angels of the Lord" have come down to Earth to relate to us? Are the messengers spiritual, physical or both? Is the message itself tarnished, distorted or altered in any way, whether the messenger arrives in an ethereal cloud, a chariot of fire . . . or an electromagnetically powered, metallic craft from a neighboring star?

PART THREE

THE CONNECTION

Chapter 12

And so they left, and on their way they saw the same star they had seen in the East. When they saw it, how happy they were, what joy was theirs! It went ahead of them until it stopped over the place where the child was. (Matthew 2: 9 - 10)

We saw an extraordinarily large star shining among the stars of heaven, and so out shined all the other stars, that they became not visible. (The Apocrypha. Protovangelion 15: 7)

So the wise men began their travel, and look, the star which they saw in the east went before them, until it came and stood over the cave where the young child was with Mary his mother. (The Apocrypha. Protovangelion 15: 9)

For the past two thousand years, scientific scholars and theologians have debated the source of the Star of Bethlehem. Among the many theories offered are, a comet, a meteor, the planet Venus, a supernova, the alignment of planets, and even a lunar eclipse of the planet Jupiter.

This last one is puzzling, as an eclipse of a heavenly body, by it's very definition, blocks out the light from its surface - not intensifies it. The planet Venus certainly is the brightest star in the sky, and, depending on its proximity to Earth during its orbit of the Sun, at times will appear even brighter. However, it would be safe to assume that even the astronomers of two thousand years ago, though their knowledge of the heavens was limited, were familiar with this star and would not mistake its usual appearance for a sign from God of the impending birth of the Messiah. Not only would a meteor move far too fast for the wise men to follow, but it would not make a screeching halt over any given landmark. A comet appears as a white streak in the sky, not as a star, and it stops for nothing unless in a collision with another heavenly body. The alignment of planets - and certainly a supernova - might outshine all the other stars in the sky but not to the point that "they became not visible." Nor would it appear to move across the sky and stop on a dime.

In any of the aforementioned theories, such celestial phenomena would be visible to King Herod, who sent the wise men to find the newborn Jesus, because of his close proximity to Bethlehem. Herod, however, did not see the star as the wise men had reported, suggesting that the object in question was much closer to the Earth.

Most of the modern-day clergy have reasoned, in light of our increasing knowledge of the universe, that the Star of Bethlehem is strictly symbolic. (Another "nonevent.") Not to detract from the existence of Jesus, nor His rightful place in theological lore, but simply a myth created to emphasis the importance of His birth. It is widely considered that most, if not all, scriptures dealing with inexplicable phenomena that defy modern laws of physics, are likewise symbolic. This would include the "pillar of cloud and fire," the parting of the Red Sea, the burning bush and Ezekiel's vision, just to name a few. If this is the case, at what point do we stop disavowing scriptures as fact? How many Biblical passages describe instances that are known to be physically impossible? Yet, these seemingly miraculous events are reported as gospel by honest witnesses in the only manner they knew to relate them. Similar to a child relating a magic trick that he had seen - he can only report the visual effect without knowing the mechanics behind it.

Let's assume, then, that the wise men were accurately reporting what they actually saw. As astronomers of their day, they knew what to expect to see in the night sky - the moon and the stars. No airplanes, helicopters, blimps, weather balloons or "swamp gas" - just the moon and the stars. They knew what the moon looked like and this object certainly wasn't that. This round, luminous object then could only be described as a "star." A star that traveled close to the Earth, slowly enough that it could be followed by men on camels, stopped and hovered over the place where Jesus lay and concentrated its light directly down upon one particular area. The fact of the matter is simply that stars do not behave in this manner.

The Star of Bethlehem was an unidentified flying object in the truest definition of the term. Whether or not it was an extraterrestrial craft, as we observe the term today, remains to be seen. A twentieth century UFO will *commonly* behave in this manner. The typical UFO report will consist of a bright light in the night sky moving slowly, silently, then hovering motionlessly for a time. Then a powerful white or bluish-white light will beam down from it to the ground.

On Sept. 7, 1984, in the skies over Minsk, Russia, two sets of air crewmen, flying in opposite directions, simultaneously witnessed a bright UFO emitting a powerful beam down to the ground and another toward the aircraft. The cockpits of both planes were illuminated with this blinding light. All of the crewmen suffered from radiation poisoning after the incident. (Reminiscent of the Cash-Landrum case, mentioned in chapter 4.)

On Nov. 5, 1975, Travis Walton and six of his companions were driving through the Apache-Sitgreaves National Forest in Arizona. It was shortly after sunset when they noticed a golden glow in the distance. Believing it to be a forest fire, they continued in its direction. They soon came upon a disk-shaped metallic object hovering silently about 15 feet in the air over a clearing about 90 feet from their truck. Walton, the front seat passenger, shouted for the driver to stop. When he did, Walton jumped out of the truck and ran toward the object. His startled friends, sensing danger, yelled at him to come back. Ignoring their warnings, Travis stood under the object for several seconds. Without warning, a blinding bluish-green light shot from the bottom of the craft, knocking him to the ground. In horror, the driver instinctively sped off.

They had gotten only a quarter of a mile down the road when they gathered their senses, stopped and turned around to go back for their friend. As they did, they saw a bright light streak through the sky from the point where they had seen the UFO. When they returned to the clearing, there was no sign of the object or Walton.

Travis Walton was missing for five days (one of the longest durations of alien abduction on record). During that period, his six companions were subjected to polygraph tests, as authorities, disbelieving their outlandish account of the incident, suspected foul play. The tests proved that all had related the truth as they believed it to be. The authorities conducted an extensive search of the area in question, without yielding so much as a clue. Five days after the abduction, Travis phoned a family member from a nearby phone booth, where they found him, frightened and disoriented. He too was subjected to polygraph tests which he successfully passed.

Of the five days of his ordeal, he was able to consciously recall only about one hour. He had woken up in a room that he at first mistook for a hospital. That notion was dashed when he was confronted by three typical greys. Unlike most abduction reports, he was not paralyzed. He leaped off the examination table and laid his hands on the first thing he could find that looked like it would serve as a weapon - a "rod-like object," as he had described it. Threateningly waving the object at the trio, they quickly retreated from the room. Walton left the room and hurried down a corridor where he was confronted by another being. This one, however, was human! At least he appeared to be human, which served to calm him down (as much as could be possible under such conditions). The man stood more than six feet tall with brown eyes and golden-brown hair.

The man didn't speak to Travis but led him into another room where three other men, who looked like the first, made him lie down on a table, placed what appeared to be an oxygen mask over his face and, once again, he lost consciousness. His next conscious memory was awakening about midnight, five days after the incredible event began, lying on mother Earth, watching the UFO streak off into the night sky.

Travis' ordeal was related in his book, "Fire in The Sky; The Walton Experience." It was also the subject of the 1993 motion picture, "Fire in The Sky." As of this writing, none of the seven participants in this event have ever deviated from their original claims.

In the fall of 1994, Trumble County, Ohio, fell under siege by three low flying UFOs. Shortly after midnight, Roy Ann Rudolph, the police dispatcher of Liberty Township, began receiving calls from local citizens about a strange, silent, brilliantly-lit craft traveling at treetop level down their residential streets. Rudolph radioed Officer Steven Remner and Sgt. Toby Meloro, who were in a local diner at the time, to ask them to investigate. Sgt. Meloro, an eight-year veteran of the force, left his partner to investigate the call. As he approached the area in question, he was hailed by a citizen, walking his dog, who reiterated the claim. Meloro drove on in search of a low-flying aircraft or helicopter which he felt certain was the cause of the complaints. When he got to a secluded area, his police cruiser shut down as if the battery had suddenly been disconnected. He looked up to see the underside of a disk-shaped metallic craft hovering silently above him, at treetop level, like a brilliant huge canopy. The center of the object bore a bright white light while the outside ring slowly rotated with alternating red, yellow, blue and green lights. He tried to notify the dispatcher on his police radio only to find it as dead as the rest of the vehicle. Not even his hand-held radio would respond. Sgt. Meloro exited the vehicle and stood beside it. As he looked up, he found himself spotlighted with a blinding white light from the object's center. After a short time, the light was extinguished, and the craft slowly and silently moved on. As it departed the scene, his cruiser started up again by itself. He jumped back into the car and tried to follow the object. He found he was able to contact the dispatcher on the radio and excitedly reported the incident.

By this time Rudolph had received more calls from concerned citizens and other police officers were involved in the vigil. Other nearby counties began phoning in similar reports.

Lieutenant James Baker of the Brookfield Township Police Department, armed with binoculars, climbed an old radar tower (reportedly the highest structure in Trumble County) to find three identical UFOs in the night sky. They were of the same description as those reported all over the county that night. By Baker's observations, as they hovered silently in the sky, the lights on their outer rings changed from red to green to yellow to blue in unison. Lieutenant Baker stood watching this orchestrated light show while saying into his police radio, "Oh God, please let these be planes." A few minutes later, his prayer for a conventional solution was denied when the trio shot off at breakneck speed from a complete standstill and vanished into the blackness of the sky.

The Liberty Township dispatcher had phoned the FAA control tower at a nearby airport to ask if they had a visual on the objects. She was informed by the Air Traffic Control operator on duty that he had neither a visual sighting nor a radar return of any unidentified aircraft in the area. After the incident a request was filed with the FAA through the Freedom of Information Act to learn the identity of the Air Traffic Control officer on duty that night. Their request was denied. Captain John Keytack of the nearby Air Reserve Base unequivocally denied any knowledge of experimental aircraft in the sky from his base that evening.

The Trumble County incident was profiled in an NBC special, "Confirmation: The Hard Evidence of Aliens Among Us?" The sequence, of course, was a dramatic re-enactment. However, it featured the actual officers involved in the case and the UFO visual effects were based on the descriptions given by hundreds of witnesses.

Of course, the mainstream scientific skeptic was afforded equal time to offer a "common sense, prosaic explanation." Astronomer James E. McGaha spoke to the television audience as one would to a small child. "This is a classic example of 'scintillation'," he casually explained. Scintillation is the twinkling effect of stars as seen through the earth's atmosphere. Often a star will not only twinkle but will appear to change color as it does so. The intense bright light was a "fireball or meteor." The fact that Sgt. Meloro's squad car died at that particular point in time was merely a "coincidence." McGaha didn't doubt the sincerity of the witnesses, but it was obviously a case of untrained observers witnessing something they couldn't explain and drawing fantastic conclusions. (If people find the accounts of UFO witnesses and alien abductees hard to believe, they should hear some of the explanations offered by the skeptics!)

In this writer's opinion, it is the highest form of insult to assume that the residents of Trumble County, Ohio, would not recognize a twinkling star in the night sky. A meteor would sport a long fiery tail, zip through the sky and be gone in a matter of seconds. It does not plod slowly down residential streets at treetop level, stopping only to direct its light on police cars. Furthermore, it would have been observed and reported by people throughout the Midwest - if not most of the country - not just in Trumble County, Ohio. It is clear that the description of the three objects reported that evening meet none of McGaha's criteria.

A dead cell in an automobile battery will prevent one from starting the vehicle but, once it is running, it will usually continue to do so until it is manually shut off. A battery will die on occasion but, once it does, it will not start up again without human intervention. Sgt. Meloro was standing outside the vehicle when the car restarted. Not only did the police car die and reactivate by itself, while in close proximity of the UFO, so did the hand-held radio that the officer had in his possession. More coincidence?

The coincidence is that cars, as well as other battery operated and electrical devices, have consistently been reported to completely shut down during a close encounter UFO sighting, then miraculously start up by themselves when the object has departed the scene.

It is also coincidental that the description of the UFO in this event (and many other incidents like it) echoes that of the wise men who followed a heavenly light to a stable in Bethlehem. I find it ironic that an astronomer of today, like the astronomers of two thousand years ago, would regard this same phenomenon as a "star."

The fact is that most astronomers have seen these unconventional objects in the sky. They have been photographed by the Hubble telescope and by our weather and spy satellites. They have been observed and photographed by American astronauts and Russian cosmonauts. Most of them keep silent about their find, yet others share their findings with civilian UFO groups such as MUFON. This way they are able to get the truth out to the public, allow photographic specialists to analyze the evidence, and still maintain their reputable standing within the scientific community.

Then there are the "qualified professionals" who risk it all in an effort to get the word out to the public that we are not alone. Major Gordon Cooper, one of the original Mercury astronauts, testified before the United Nations. The following is an excerpt from his sworn testimony:

(Major Gordon Cooper): "I believe that these extraterrestrial vehicles and their crews are visiting this planet from other planets . . . Most astronauts are reluctant to discuss UFOs." "I did have occasion in 1951 to have two days of observation, of many flights of them of different sizes flying in fighter formation, generally from east to west over Europe."

In a taped interview by J. L. Ferrando, Major Cooper said: "For many years I have lived with a secret, in a secrecy imposed on all specialists in astronautics. I can now reveal that every day, in the USA, our radar instruments capture objects of a form and composition unknown to us. And there are thousands of witness reports and a quantity of documents to prove this, but nobody wants to make them public. Why? Because the authorities are afraid that people may think of God knows what kind of horrible invader. So the password still is, 'we have to avoid panic by all means.'

"I was, furthermore, a witness to an extraordinary phenomenon here on this planet Earth. It happened a few months ago in Florida. There I saw with my own eyes a defined area of ground being consumed by flames, with four indentations left by a flying object which had descended in the middle of a field. Beings had left the craft . . . there were other traces to prove that. They seemed to have studied topography. They had collected soil samples and, eventually, they returned to where they had come from, disappearing at enormous speed. I happen to know that authorities did just about everything to keep this incident from the press and TV, in fear of a panicky reaction from the public."

In June of 1965, Ed White, the first American to walk in space, and James McDivitt were over Hawaii while orbiting the Earth in a Gemini spacecraft, when they spotted a disk-shaped UFO with long arms protruding from it. McDivitt took some pictures of the object with a cine-camera. Needless to say, those photographs have never been released.

In December of the same year, James Lovell and Frank Borman, on their second orbit of a fourteen-day flight, observed several UFOs some distance from their capsule. Gemini control at Cape Kennedy suggested that they were seeing the final stage of their own Titan booster rocket. Borman advised control that they could see the booster rocket - that this was something completely different. The following is an excerpt from the taped conversation between Lovell and Gemini control:

Lovell: Bogey at ten o'clock high.
Control: This is Houston. Say again 7.
Lovell: Said we have a bogey at ten o'clock high.
Control: Gemini 7, is that the booster or an actual sighting?
Lovell: We have several . . . actual sightings.
Control: Estimated distance or size?
Lovell: We also have the booster in sight . . .

Commander Eugene Cernan of the Apollo 17 mission, stated in a 1973 article in the Los Angeles Times, "I've been asked about UFOs and I've said publicly I thought they were somebody else . . . some other civilization."

Pilot Walter Schirra, of the Mercury 8 flight, is credited with coining the code word "Santa Claus" to indicate the sighting of a flying saucer near a space capsule. It was probably Schirra's attempt to draw a correlation between two presumably nonexistent entities. It seemed to work well at first. No one seemed to notice when a "Santa Claus" was reported. However, by the flight of Apollo 8, when James Lovell came out from behind the moon and reported to the world, "Please be informed that there is a Santa Claus," many people, who had heard that term from astronauts in the past, began to suspect a hidden meaning.

On that historic day, July 21, 1969, shortly after man first set foot on the moon, the entire world listened in on a live transmission between Neil Armstrong, and Edwin "Buzz" Aldrin (on the lunar surface) and Mission Control. Armstrong had seen a strong light coming from the ridge of a crater and went to investigate. Forgetting (or not caring) that the transmission was being broadcast live globally, he began describing what appeared to be two brightly illuminated UFOs on the moon watching the astronauts. The written transcript of the interchange does not reflect the excitement and disbelief of the astronauts nor the panicked earthbound controller trying frantically to get Armstrong to shut up, break transmission and go to a secure frequency.

The following is the transcript of the conversation between Armstrong, Aldrin and Houston Control, heard globally, before public transmission went black:

Armstrong: Ha! What is it?

Aldrin: We have some explanation for that?

Houston: We have not. Don't worry, continue your program!

Armstrong: Oh boy! It's a . . . it's . . . it . . . it is really something . . . similar to . . . fantastic here! You . . . you could never imagine this!

Houston: Roger. We know about that. Could you go the other way? Go back the other way!

Armstrong: Well, it's kind of rigged! Ha! Pretty spectacular! God, what is that there? It's hollow! What the hell is that?!

Houston: Go Tango! Tango!

Armstrong: Ha! There's kind of a light there now!

Houston: Roger, we got it! We watched it! Lose communication! Bravo Tango! Bravo Tango! Select Jezebel! Jezebel!

Armstrong: Ya' . . . ha! But this is unbelievable!

Houston: We call you up Bravo Tango! Bravo Tango!

Even though worldwide communication ceased at this point, unnamed radio hams, using VHF receiving facilities, were able to bypass NASA's broadcasting outlets, and recorded the following transmission:

Houston: What's there? Mission control calling Apollo 11...

Armstrong: These babies are huge, sir! Enormous! Oh my God! You wouldn't believe it! I'm telling you there are other spacecraft out there, lined up on the far side of the crater edge! They're on the moon watching us!

A former NASA employee, Otto Binder, later confirmed this transmission. Armstrong later confirmed that this story was true and admitted that the CIA was behind the cover-up. He stated that they (the astronauts) were "warned off" by the aliens. When asked what that meant, he replied, "I can't go into details, except to say that their ships were far superior to ours both in size and technology. Boy, were they big! And menacing! No, there is no question of a space station."

When challenged with the fact that NASA had other missions after Apollo 11, Armstrong replied, "Naturally - NASA was committed at that time and couldn't risk panic on Earth. But it really was a scoop and then back again."

In 1979 Maurice Chatelain, former chief of NASA Communications Systems, confirmed the stories of Armstrong's UFO sightings on the moon saying, "The encounter was common knowledge in NASA, but nobody has talked about it until now. All Apollo and Gemini flights were followed, both at a distance and sometimes also quite closely, by space vehicles of extraterrestrial origin - flying saucers, or UFOs - if you want to call them by that name. Every time it occurred, the astronauts informed Mission Control, who then ordered absolute silence."

And yet, the vocal mainstream skeptics (an estimated 90% of whom know the difference) continue trying to dazzle the "untrained observers" with words like, "scintillation," "fireballs" and "coincidence." If they wish to perpetuate the cover-up, their purpose would be better served by remaining silent, as opposed to insulting the intelligence of the world's population by offering nonsensical explanations that, in no way, correspond with the evidence.

At the beginning of this chapter, two passages were mentioned from the Apocrypha. These are scriptures that were expunged from the King James Authorized Version of the Bible in 1796. Etymologically the word "Apocrypha" means, "that which is hidden." Which begs the question, "why were these certain scriptures hidden?" Some believe that these passages are too mysterious and profound to be communicated to anyone except the initiated. Others feel that they were withdrawn from the Bible because the messages they communicated were heretical. The church fathers have been poring over the Holy Scriptures from the time they first came to light until the present. It would appear that, as with the expulsion of passages directly referring to the concept of reincarnation, many other scriptures conveyed truths that did not reflect the world view that the church wished to convey. Once again, if one will consider all Biblical passages, complete with "that which is hidden," fused with today's scientific knowledge, we will soon see the Star of Bethlehem and all of its forerunners in a completely different perspective.

In Fig. 7, we see an artist's rendition of the nativity. This painting was produced during the renaissance period. Notice the object in the sky over Mary's left shoulder and the man in the background looking up at it. What could have inspired this artist to paint such a rendition of the birth of Jesus? Is this another example, like the stone carvings of ancient astronauts, of our ancestors dabbling in science fiction? Or is this an accurate depiction of what had been witnessed so many years before and passed on from generation to generation? Could this painting reflect the true nativity scene *before* western orthodoxy took the more detailed description of the event and "hid" it in the Apocrypha?

Marc Davenport, in his book "Visitors From Time" (mentioned in Chapter 3), suggests that UFOs are time machines from our own future. He states that, in such a vehicle, future astronauts would be able to travel back in time to witness great events . . . like the birth of Christ. It is not a great leap to take this as an implication that the Star of Bethlehem was a time machine, from our own future, come to observe the birth of the Messiah. However, given the Bible's history of human intervention by the occupants of these "heavenly vehicles," it would logically follow that the purpose of this bright, slow-moving object, was more than that of observation.

Chapter 13

Two things have thus far been established: (1.) The people of that era revered UFOs as God or messengers of God. (2.) Mary (being a virgin and having been personally informed by one of these messengers) believed she had been impregnated by God.

Before continuing with this hypothesis, it would do well to give a brief synopsis on some of the more common elements related to the average alien abduction experience for the benefit of those less familiar with the scenario. Scriptural correlations will be added where applicable.

It is a common misconception among the skeptical that many people have fed off the delusions of the few. Viz., a handful of people originally reported being abducted by aliens, taken for a ride in a "flying saucer" and returned. Upon learning of these claims, others either invented or imagined similar claims. In fact, as in the case of the NDE, many people, from every corner of the globe, originally reported such abductions but the cases were kept guarded as the ravings of the mentally infirm. It wasn't until the volume of reports reached that of phenomenal proportion that notes were compared and a criterion established to weed out actual abduction victims from publicity seekers.

Although most abductions occur at night, while the victim is in bed, there have been many reports of waking and daylight abductions. (Betty and Barny Hill and the Travis Walton experience, previously mentioned, are just two such cases in point.) This fact, coupled with multi-witness abductions, eliminates the "dream" theory as an exclusive explanation. In the case of nocturnal abductions, the victim will see a blinding white or bluish-white light show in through their window, or simply appear within a closed room.

Then a bright cloud overshadowed the cave and the midwife said, "this day my soul is magnified for mine eyes have seen surprising things and salvation is brought forth to Israel. But on a sudden, the cloud became a great light in the cave, so that their

109

eyes could not bear it. But the light gradually decreased until the infant appeared and sucked the breast of his mother Mary. (The Apocrypha. Protevangelion 14:10-12)

And behold, it (the cave) was all filled with lights, greater than the light of lamps and candles, and greater than the light of the Sun itself. (The Apocrypha. 1 Infancy 1:10)

The Apocryphal scriptures make mention of the Star of Bethlehem in much greater detail than the first books of the New Testament. Here again are the "cloud" and great light that had become synonymous with "the Glory of the Lord." This abnormally bright and unearthly light had filled the cave in which Mary had been hidden by Joseph. He then left her in labor to go into the city to find a midwife for assistance. The New Testament has given the impression that Jesus was born in the stable because there was no room in the inn. The Apocrypha plainly states that Jesus was born in a cave, then moved to the stable afterwards. It was not for lack of room in the inn that they ended up in a stable, but for the fact that Herod was searching for them with the intent of killing the child.

Humanoid beings will *float* through a closed widow or wall and stand by the victim's bed. In modern ufology, the beings are described as about four to four and a half feet tall, greyish-white skin, a large head that is out of proportion to their bodies (by human standards) and large black, almond-shaped eyes. However, as mentioned in a previous chapter, there are the "Nordic types," who appear human in every respect, that are seen once the victim is aboard the craft. As more information is garnered, it appears that "greys" are a subordinate race (perhaps clones) that abduct victims for the purpose of a superior race.

Although stone carvings and paintings of both the typical large-eyed greys and very human looking ancient astronauts exist from thousands of years ago, the Biblical visitors were strictly that of the "human" variety.

Although most abductees require the aid of hypnosis to recall their experiences, many have conscious memories of their ordeal, and become accustomed to the visitor's occasional intrusion.

Accordingly going into her, he filled the chamber where she was with a prodigious light, and in a most courteous manner saluting her. (The Apocrypha: Mary 7: 2)

But the virgin, who had before been well acquainted with the countenances of angels, and whom such light from heaven was no uncommon thing, was neither terrified with the vision of the angel, nor astonished at the greatness of the light, but only troubled about the angel's words. (The Apocrypha: Mary 7: 4 - 5)

Abductees usually find themselves in a temporary state of paralysis. Invariably, the aliens will communicate to the subject, telepathically, that they are not to be afraid. They assure them that they are not going to hurt them. This usually does little to comfort the abductee. At this point, they will lay their *four-fingered* hand upon the subject's forehead, resulting in a calming and sometimes euphoric effect.

In Korbach, Germany, on February 18, 1990, a woman was walking her dog about 6:00 P.M., when she witnessed a disk-shaped object hovering overhead. It emitted a strong bluish-white light that engulfed her. She heard a voice (whether audibly or telepathically is unknown) saying, "Don't be afraid. Nothing bad will happen to you."

The angel said to her, "Don't be afraid, Mary: God has been gracious to you." (Luke 1: 30)

An angel of the Lord appeared to them, and the glory shown over them. They were terribly afraid, but the angel said to them, "Don't be afraid! I am here with good news for you, which will bring great joy to all the people." (Luke 2: 9-10)

When I saw him, I fell down at his feet like a dead man. He placed his right hand on me and said "Don't be afraid! I am the first and the last." (Revelation 1: 17)

Biblical passages that refer to angels attempting to comfort witnesses with, "Don't be afraid," or "Fear not," are far too numerous to outline here. Anyone familiar with scripture, however, will readily agree that this is a common statement for them to make.

The victim is then *levitated* off the bed and, along with their abductors, ascended up and *through* the closed window or wall, as if it wasn't there, to the waiting ship.

In Budd Hopkins' book, "Witnessed," an exhaustive investigation into a Brooklyn, N.Y., abduction case, yielded testimonial evidence from several witnesses to the actual abduction. On Nov. 30, 1989, at about 3:00 A.M., Linda Cortile (a pseudonym), a veteran abductee, was abducted from her twelfth-story apartment by three greys in the aforementioned manner. At least three cars traveling on the Brooklyn Bridge stopped functioning at the same moment. (In the same manner as Sgt. Meloro's squad car mentioned in the previous chapter.) All of the occupants got out of their vehicles to witness a disk-shaped UFO hovering silently over a nearby city street. The craft emitted a strong bluish-white light that was directed at Cortile's twelfth-story window. As they watched, to their amazement, a woman in a long, white nightgown, accompanied by three small greys, floated through the window and up to the waiting craft. The light was then extinguished and the UFO sped off, plunging into the East River.

As a result of his investigations, Hopkins found more than twenty independent witnesses who viewed the incident from different angles. Among them were a police officer, two U.S. Government Intelligence/Security officers and an unnamed foreign Head of State who's anonymity, for obvious reasons, was preserved.

The power of the Lord came upon me with great force and as his spirit carried me off, I felt bitter and angry. So I came to Tel Abib beside the Chebar River, where the exiles were living and for seven days I stayed there, overcome by what I had seen and heard. (Ezekiel 3: 14, 16)

What if the spirit of the Lord carries you off to some unknown place as soon as I leave? (1 Kings 18: 12)

They kept talking as they walked on; Then suddenly a chariot of fire pulled by horses of fire came between them, and Elijah was taken up to heaven by a whirlwind. (2 Kings 2: 11)

Where did the "winged angel" concept come from? The Bible speaks of angels descending from and ascending to a brilliantly illuminated cloud. Nowhere does it speak of "wings" being a part of their anatomy. In Isaiah 6: 1 -7, Isaiah allegedly witnessed "flaming creatures," each having six wings, that he assumed were angels. These were referred to as "*Seraphim.*" Ezekiel's vision included "living beings" with four wings that he too felt must be angels. These were referred to as "Cherubim." These "beings" never spoke to Ezekiel though. They seemed to be responsible for lifting and landing the attached object above them. As discussed in chapter 3, these "Cherubim" were most likely the legs of an unknown craft with helicopter-type propellers for the purpose of maneuvering about after landing. However, artists' renditions of angels invariably attach two wings to these heavenly messengers.

One alien abductee, in describing the typical grey, emphatically stated that her captor had wings! When the investigator asked her if she had actually seen wings on the being, she replied, "No, I didn't see wings . . . but he was floating around the room in midair. He must have had wings!"

It is this reasoning (logical as it may seem) that has fostered the belief that angels *must* have wings. How else could they descend from and ascend to the sky? Artists have employed this reasoning to depict the heavenly messengers and to differentiate them from the earthbound humans within the scene. In actuality, the same anti-gravitational properties responsible for the craft's maneuverability are within the light, enabling the levitation of biological forms within its beam.

As to the seemingly impossible notion that solid objects cannot simply pass through other solid objects unscathed, quantum theory acknowledges the possibility, although they are, to date, unable to devise a device for its practical application. Grade-school science has taught us that all matter comprises billions of tiny atoms. Each atom may be compared to our own solar system. An atom's nucleus, comprising protons and neutrons, is comparable to our own Sun. Electrons whirl around the nucleus as do our planets, albeit, at about the speed of light. Between these electrons is open space. It is the positive electrical charge of the proton and the negative electrical charge of the electron that holds this atom together like a magnet. (The neutron is so named because it is neutral - having no electric charge.) When two solid objects come together, it is this electric magnetism that prevents the two from merging. It is similar to placing the positive poles of two magnets together. They repel each other.

If, however, the polarity of the atoms in one object were reversed and the other left alone, there would be no repulsion. The void spaces between the electrons in both objects would allow the atoms of both objects to merge as one or pass through each other.

Given UFOs are thought to employ electromagnetic propulsion systems, evidenced by their effect upon automobiles, electrical devices and the earth's gravitational pull, it is no great leap to assume that the same technology is employed to affect reverse polarization within that "prodigious light" that is so often witnessed.

Though some abductions have been witnessed by others, most often others nearby appear to be "switched off." When the victim is in bed at the onset of the event, they will try to arouse their spouse or others in the household. Every one of them will continue to sleep as if having been drugged. It would appear that the intruders employ this unknown technique to assure the least number of witnesses as well as the least amount of resistance.

When the abduction takes place where there are a number of conscious potential witnesses, it has been reported that those who are not participants in the event are placed in a state of suspended animation. Although such claims are not as prevalent and considered by investigators to be of "high-strangeness," they do occur.

Linda Cortile, in the aforementioned Brooklyn Bridge abduction, recalled under hypnosis being taken by three very human looking beings as a child of ten or eleven, while on a family outing to a swimming pool at Brooklyn's Coney Island. She had gone into the bathhouse to change into her swimsuit when she was confronted by three male figures, whose occasional presence she had become accustomed to. They simply told her, "It's time to go." After some resistance on her part, she felt compelled to acquiesce. The men led her out of the bathhouse to the waiting ship that hovered overhead. As she walked past the swimming pool, she noted an eerie silence. Many people were in and about the pool as she passed - but they were *frozen* in place! The children in the pool, who had been splashing water on each other, were as mannequins frozen in position. Big droplets of water remained suspended in midair above their heads. People that they passed on their way were rooted in mid-stride. It was like walking through a three-dimensional photograph.

A similar scene was reported by Joseph, after leaving Mary in the cave to go to Bethlehem to secure a midwife. This passage was one of those extracted from the Bible and "hidden" in the Apocrypha:

But as I was going (said Joseph) I looked up into the air and I saw the clouds astonished, and the fowls of the air stopping in the midst of their flight. And I looked down towards the earth and saw a table spread, and working people sitting around it, but their hands were upon the table and they did not move to eat. They who had meat in their mouths did not eat. They who lifted their hands up to their heads did not draw them back. And they who lifted them up to their mouths did not put anything in, but all their faces were fixed upwards. And I beheld the sheep dispersed and yet the sheep stood still. And the shepherd lifted up his hand to smite them and his hand continued up. And I looked unto a river and saw the kids with their mouths close to the water and touching it, but they did not drink. (Protevangelion 13: 1-10)

This would account for reports of "missing time" by those in the vicinity of abduction activity. One moment it is 1:00 P.M. and the next it is 3:30 P.M. More often it is the abductee that reports missing time, as in the Betty and Barney Hill case. It is a most unsettling experience to be doing something in one room of the house one minute, and your next conscious recollection is two hours later . . . in another room . . . with your shirt on backwards! Often only regression with the aid of a professional hypnotist can one break through that wall of amnesia and fill in the blanks. (Inevitably to the horror of the disbelieving subject.)

The most common event in the abduction process is that of a thorough physical examination conducted by the beings. The victim is placed on a flat, hard table and examined from head to foot. In most cases, sperm is extracted from the male and ova from the female. A football-shaped, metal object with a mechanical eye in the front, will slowly pass over and around the body, apparently scanning or taking X-rays of it. Then an instrument is pushed up a nostril until a "crunching" sound is heard. Once the abductees have been returned, they will begin to experience chronic nosebleeds that were, hitherto, nonexistent. When the abductee seeks medical attention, X-rays will show a tiny foreign object embedded in the cartilage at the base of the nasal passage near the skull.

The unprecedented nosebleeds made for easy detection on the part of the abductees and their doctors. It may well be for this reason that the aliens began implanting these devices in other locations of the body. Implants have been found in the legs, arms and hands. Sometimes the device will be implanted at the base of the skull next to the medulla oblongata, which renders it impossible to be removed surgically. On occasion, an implant will appear on an X-ray and a future appointment will be set for its removal. In the interim, the patient will be re-abducted and the implant removed. To the amazement of the physician, further X-rays reveal the absence of the object with no evidence of any surgical procedure having been employed.

When an implant *is* removed, it is typically found to be a pebble-like structure about one eighth to one quarter of inch in diameter, although some others are clear, glass-like shards. Though a small percentage have been found to be mundane terrestrial objects, such as glass or wood splinters or a cyst, most are determined to be *not* of a physiological or even terrestrial nature. The implant is covered with a thin membrane comprising the patient's own tissue, assumed to be for the purpose of preventing the body's natural defense mechanism from rejecting it. The composition of this membrane is so dense that it cannot be severed with a surgeon's scalpel.

When subjected to laboratory examination, the implant is found to posses a carbon/silicon base, both of which are elements of this and many other planets. Other elements found within this suspicious object, however, are not found on any element table known to man! This fact makes the alien implant one of the most convincing forms of physical evidence in the ufologist's arsenal.

Mankind thinks nothing of anaesthetizing an animal in the wild, tagging it and affixing a collar around its neck that will allow researchers to monitor its physical vital signs and track its every move via a satellite. They may then locate the animal at a later date and repeat the procedure. With the advancement of miniaturization of computer technology, researchers will soon employ a single chip, implanted under the skin of the beast, to accomplish the same result. What a sobering and horrific epiphany it would be to find that this very technology has been employed for thousands of years by extraterrestrials with humans as their test subjects!

It is usually found, through investigation, that alien abductions follow genetic lines. If one is an abductee, chances are great that one or both of their parents were abductees. Chances are equally as great that their children, as well as other family members, will also be unwilling participants in the same phenomenon.

The Apocryphal book of Mary (chapter two) recounts the appearance of an angel who came to Mary's parents, Joachem and Anna, on separate occasions, before Mary's conception, in that same "prodigious light." He first told them not to be afraid and not to confuse him with a spirit. He told them that even though Anna was barren, she would conceive a child whom they must name Mary. The angel went on to tell them that Mary would give birth to a child while she was yet a virgin and his name would be Jesus.

Shortly before Mary became pregnant with Jesus, her cousin Elizabeth and her husband Zechariah, was also approached separately by an angel. (The same light - the same "don't be afraid.") The couple, as were Mary's parents, were both old and Elizabeth was barren. Nonetheless, Elizabeth was told that she would conceive a child who must be named John. (Luke 1: 5 - 23)

When the angel spoke to Mary, he said, *Remember your relative Elizabeth. It is said that she cannot have children but she herself is now six months pregnant, even though she is very old.* (Luke 1: 36)

It is obvious that visitations by these "heavenly agents" were prevalent in Jesus' lineage.

Many women who claim abduction experiences have become pregnant whether they are married, single, sexually active or not. The pregnancy will be confirmed by a gynecologist within the first trimester. Within three to four months after conception, they will suffer a miscarriage. Unlike most miscarriages, however, no fetal tissue is to be found. In fact, there is no evidence that they had ever been pregnant.

Abduction victims almost always describe being escorted by the aliens through a large room aboard the craft, where there are many cylindrical, transparent canisters filled with some type of liquid. In the center of each is a premature fetus with large black eyes. The tour of this bizarre incubation room is thought to be an attempt, on the part of the visitors, to show the abductee the purpose of their mission. They have also been shown holographic images of the Earth undergoing global, natural catastrophes. The aliens have communicated to their victims that they are genetically engineering a race of beings for the purpose of repopulating our planet in the event of such a disaster. They warn that, through pollution and the detonation of atomic weapons, man is hastening his own demise.

After repeated abductions (and at least one mysterious miscarriage), the female abductee will be handed a small child and told that it is *hers*. These children are described as small, listless humans with frail limbs, white, wispy hair, a pointed chin and larger-than-normal black eyes. The beings will then leave mother and child alone, for a time, in the hope that the mother will bond with and nurture the child.

In Budd Hopkins' book, "Intruders," he relates a case where a thirteen-year-old girl underwent an abortion. The girl insisted that she had not had sexual intercourse. It was found that her hymen was still intact. She was still a virgin! Under hypnosis, the girl recounted an alien abduction experience when she was artificially inseminated. She described her abductors as the typical small, grey, large black almond-shaped eyed aliens.

This is not to suggest in any way that Jesus was a human/alien hybrid of *this* race. It is, however, to *strongly* suggest that he *was* a human/alien hybrid of the "Nordic" type (or another completely human race). The same race that Ezekiel identified as "men." The same race as those who were revered as "angels" - human in appearance, albeit having the ability to descend from and ascend to a brilliantly illuminated "cloud."

But is hybridization between humans and *any* alien race even a possibility?

In the September 1998 issue of Mutual UFO Network's UFO Journal, a reader, in his published letter to the editor, begged to differ with the human/alien hybridization theory. Malcolm Smith, who holds two degrees in the field of zoology, stated, "A host of factors prevents hybridization between all but very closely related species." He goes on to say that, even though different earthly species have different appearances, they all share the same fundamental structure. Humans and lower animals share the same genetic code. The biochemical makeups between man and lower animals, are simply variations on the same theme. That doesn't mean that hybridization between a dog and a human could be accomplished. Not even with the technique of in vitro fertilization.

Smith went on to make the assumption that an alien's organs would certainly not be constructed similarly to any earthly species. Its DNA code would be vastly different from ours. "In a cell with a different genetic code, the alien gene could not produce the chemical it was coded to produce."

In other words, "Human/alien hybridization is impossible because the DNA of humans and that of the extraterrestrial being, is not compatible." This may well be true, however, this observation may be rephrased without taking its meaning out of context, i.e., "Human/alien hybridization is impossible '*unless*' the

DNA of humans and that of the extraterrestrial beings, *'is'* compatible."

Creation stories abound throughout almost every ancient culture on the planet. Although the myths of this wondrous event may vary in content and description, the underlying theme remains constant. "The gods came down from the sky and created man, who assumed the appearance of the gods that created them." The scriptures, from which the Holy Bible is comprised, are no exception.

And God said, "Let 'us' make man in 'our' image, after 'our' likeness: and let them have dominion over the fish of the sea, and over the birds of the heavens, and over the cattle, and over all the Earth, and over every creeping thing that creepeth upon the earth." (Genesis 1: 26)

Orthodox religions teach that God made man in "*his*" image, but the scriptures clearly use the plurals, "us" and "our." To whom was God speaking?

When people had spread all over the world and daughters were being born, some of the heavenly beings saw that these young women were beautiful, so they took the ones they liked. Then the Lord said, "I will not allow people to live forever; They are mortal. From now on they will live no longer that 120 years." In those days and even later, there were giants on the Earth who were descendants of human women and the heavenly beings. They were the great heroes and famous men of long ago.

(Genesis 6: 1-4)

Numbers 13: 22, refers to a place called Hebron where the descendants of a race of giants called Anakim, lived. Actually, the Hebrew word that was translated to "giants," is "nephilum," which literally means, "those who came down." Even a text, discovered in the Dead Sea Scrolls, refers to "angels" interbreeding with human women.

In Raymond E. Fowler's book, "The Watchers: The Secret Design Behind UFO Abduction," Betty Andreasson Luca, an alien abductee since childhood, reported that her captors had once told her that they had been entrusted with and responsible for the care of all natural form "since the beginning." Betty's ongoing abduction case has proven to be one of the most well documented and celebrated cases in ufology.

Mainstream science would be the last to entertain the notion that man's beginnings were the result of "cosmic seeding" by an extraterrestrial race. Yet, as Fowler observed on page 204 of "The Watchers," they (scientists) are unable to find a link between Neanderthal and Cro-Magnon man. This is the "missing link" often referred to. The appearance of Cro-Magnon man was too soon after and too dramatic a change from its predecessor (Neanderthal) to constitute an evolutionary link. The ramification of this fact is that Homo sapiens simply sprang into being without the evolutionary process involved. In the absence of any other explanation, genetic engineering cannot be ruled out.

In John 4: 24, Jesus tells us that *"God is spirit."* The angel told Mary, *"Don't confuse me with a spirit."* But isn't this exactly what mankind has been doing since the beginning of religious doctrine? The thesaurus offers other words for God such as author, creator, father, founder, founding father, framer, generator and source. These *physical* beings, described in the Bible, have claimed to be just that - our creator. In this light, perhaps "God" is the proper term. Yet, religion holds them as spiritual beings.

Abduction victims often tell their captors that they have no right to perpetrate such an intrusion. Their retort is simply, "Yes, we do." Is it the fact that we are *their* creation that gives them such a right?

A spirit can exist on any plane of existence or outside of the earth's atmosphere. Not so in the case of a physical entity. Nor can a spirit breed with a physical entity. Therefore, if God is spirit, as Jesus insists, how could that spirit impregnate the physical body of Mary?

The soul's unification with the physical, however, is another matter. It may enter into any physical form designed to support it. The spirit of Jesus (the Son of the spiritual God) needed a physical body in which to express the truths of the spiritual plane to a primitive physical world. This was accomplished via the same means of abduction and in vitro fertilization that is vastly reported today - by the same race of beings that spawned Homo-sapiens in the beginning, making us in *their* image. Their mode of conveyance was that of one of the same UFOs described elsewhere and often in Biblical text. Although in this case, it was referred to as "the Star of Bethlehem."

Chapter 14

Orthodox Christians have often wondered why the Bible has failed to mention the activities of Christ's childhood. After His birth, He is twelve years old before a brief discussion is given about His wandering off, only to be found by His parents in the temple. The next time we hear of Him, He is a man in the last three years of His ministry before the crucifixion. Some scholars theorize that Mary, Joseph and Jesus were keeping "a low profile," as the Romans wished to seek Him out and kill Him. Herod had already shown his determination to rid Israel of the man who would be king, by summarily executing all of the infant children in Bethlehem. Thus, there were no records kept of Jesus' movements during that period. In fact, there were many scriptures depicting Jesus' activities during His infancy and childhood. But, for reasons that will soon become clear, these documents were expunged from the authorized version of the Bible. Jesus' actions as a child were totally inconsistent with the benevolent Lord that He grew to become in His maturity.

In 1 Infancy of the Apocrypha, many accounts are given of the infirm being cured by washing in the water in which the infant Jesus had been bathed. There was even an account of a man who had allegedly been turned into a mule as the result of a spell cast upon him. Mary placed Jesus on the back of the mule and he was miraculously transformed back into a man. It would seem that this story was too farfetched for the orthodox church to accept as fact. Therefore, they branded it as heretical. The average Christian today has grown up with Biblical verse that would seem too farfetched for modern scientific acceptance. Yet, they accept these stories as gospel for no other reason than the fact that they are in the Bible. Personally, I don't find this account any more inconsistent with reason and logic than turning water into wine, feeding the multitude with two fishes and five loaves of bread, bringing forth water from a stone or raising the dead. If people had grown up with the story of the man transformed into a mule and back again, they would accept it as well.

There is the story of Jesus who, after forming sparrows out of mud, orders the sculptures to fly away, whereupon, they did exactly that. Then, His abilities took a sinister turn. He was playing hide and seek with other boys. When it was Jesus' turn to find His hiding playmates, He turned them into "kids" (goats). Only at the pleadings of their mothers did He transform them back into their original form, in the presence of the disbelieving women.

One Sabbath day, Jesus and other boys were diverting water from a river to make little fish-pools. Another boy chastised them for doing so on the Sabbath and ran to break down Jesus' fish-pool. As he did, Jesus caused the water in the pool to vanish. In verse 21 of 1 Infancy, Jesus said to the boy, *"In like manner as this water has vanished, so shall thy life vanish,"* and presently the boy died.

Another time, when the Lord Jesus was coming home in the evening with Joseph, He met a boy, who ran so hard against Him, that he threw Him down. To whom the Lord Jesus said, "As thou hast thrown me down, so shalt thou fall, nor ever rise." And that moment the boy fell down and died. (1 Infancy 19: 22 - 24)

Joseph and Mary took Him to a schoolmaster to be educated. The master said to Jesus, "say Aleph" (the Hebrew equivalent to the letter A.) *And when he had said Aleph, the master bade him pronounce Beth (B); To which the Lord Jesus replied, "tell me first the meaning of the letter Aleph, and then I will pronounce Beth," But this master, when he lift up his hand to whip him, had his hand presently withered, and he died. Then said Joseph to St. Mary, "henceforth we will not allow Him to go out of the house; for everyone who displeases Him is killed."* (1 Infancy 20: 14 - 16.)

If these scriptures are accurate, (and there is no reason to assume that they are any less accurate than those that were left in the Bible) they are self-evident of the reasoning for the orthodox church to extract them. The actions of the young Jesus are certainly not suitable paradigms for a loving, merciful Lord. The obvious abuse of power displayed by Jesus, is typical of any child in an attempt to find out just what he can do and how far he can go. Needless to say, there is no precedence for this particular extent of power, but the underlying principle remains the same.

Once Jesus matured and took the full meaning of the scriptures of old to heart, he pulled in the reins, used his powers only for the good of mankind and became the benevolent Savior of His (and all) people.

No one, to my knowledge, associated with the UFO phenomenon has been reported to possess paranormal abilities to the extent that Jesus of Nazareth displayed. However, as mentioned earlier, abductees often display paranormal abilities to some extent after undergoing an alien abduction. If this hypothesis is accurate, however, we are talking about a highly-developed spiritual entity, whose physical body, the gene pool of which, was comprised between that of a highly advanced race and a woman whose family tree was rich with alien encounters. If simply being subjected to the environment of the alien presence gives birth to psychic ability, such as precognition, clairvoyance and faith-healing, the product of the aforementioned combination could, understandably, greatly enhance these abilities.

Although the Bible mentions His being found in the Temple after wandering off at the age of twelve, its descriptions of the events within the Temple are lacking. The reason for this is that they too became a part of Apocryphal text. Jesus had dazzled and confounded the priests of the Temple with His knowledge, when the topic of discussion turned to astronomy:

When a certain astronomer, who was present, asked the Lord Jesus, whether He had studied astronomy, the Lord replied and told him the number of the spheres and heavenly bodies, as also their triangular, square and sextile aspect; their progressive and retrograde motion; their size and several prognostications; and other things which the reason of man had never discovered.
(1 Infancy 21: 9, 10.)

Here is a twelve-year-old boy, schooled at home, (because of His parent's fear as to how He might use or misuse His powers) by common people with little or no knowledge of earthly matters - let alone matters of astronomy - teaching the masters as to the layout of the cosmos. From where was this knowledge garnered? In 2 Infancy 3: 6, Jesus himself admits that He was at a loss as to the source of His own knowledge.

After all the people had been baptized, Jesus also was baptized. While he was praying, heaven was opened and the holy spirit came down upon him in bodily form like a dove. And a voice came from heaven, "You are my own dear Son. I am pleased with you." (Luke 3: 21-22)

As soon as Jesus was baptized, he came up out of the water. Then heaven was opened to him, and he saw the spirit of God coming down like a dove and lighting on him. (Matthew 3: 16)

In both of these verses, witnesses reported the "heavens open," which, once again, describes the mouth of the vortex between one dimension and another. Something descended from this vortex *"like a dove."* Notice that neither Luke nor Matthew claim that an actual dove came down as in artists' interpretations but something "like a dove." This would indicate that the object's motion, in its descent, mimicked that of a dove.

There have been many UFO sightings where the witness will report a "falling leaf" pattern involved in its descent. As it descends it will sway from side to side before touching down on the earth, giving the appearance of a dove in flight. However, Matthew observed that this anomaly "lighted on" Jesus. I very much doubt that a mechanical craft would have done so. If you will recall, a light from the sky was revered as "the spirit of God." It is much more likely that this dove-like object was one of the same free-floating balls of light that were dubbed "foo-fighters" in the second World War and have been witnessed over wheat fields as crop circles are formed.

Matthew 3: 16, states that "He came up out of the water." Did this mean that He walked to the shore or was levitated straight up out of the water? Scripture is unclear as to this point. However, Jesus left the scene immediately thereafter and was not seen for the next forty days. The Bible states that He went up into the mountains to meditate, converse with His heavenly father, was tempted by an evil angel and attended to by benevolent ones. Needless to say, Jesus was not in the company of His disciples during this period, so whatever transpired must have been related to the author of the scripture by Jesus himself. Whether He walked to the shore and immediately departed for the mountains, or was taken up from the water and conveyed to the mountains, is a matter of interpretation.

But what of the voice from the sky that announced, "You are my dear Son. I am pleased with you." Could this have been telepathically imparted into the minds of those in attendance at Jesus' baptism? Or were the words audibly heard? To investigate this, let's consider the "Mount of Transfiguration."

In Matthew 17: 1 - 8, Jesus took Peter, James and John up onto a high mountain. Suddenly a change came over Jesus. His face *"shone like the Sun"* and His clothes were dazzling white. Then they saw Jesus in the presence of Moses and Elijah. Then the disciples, once again, witnessed the presence of the "shining cloud" moving over them. The disciples fell down on the ground. When they looked up again, *only* Jesus was there.

It has been established that inexplicable phenomena will often occur while in the presence of this shining cloud (then, as well as today). In this case, the disciples witnessed Moses and Elijah. These men had been dead some two thousand years. Elijah was the one that had been physically taken up into the sky in a whirlwind. Moses, however, died a natural death. How the disciples were able to identify the two men is unknown. Perhaps they were told by Jesus of their identity. In any case, there they stood conversing with Jesus. If a UFO had picked up Elijah and taken him out into the cosmos, it is possible that he could still be physically alive. It was Albert Einstein who theorized that if man could go out into space, the further out he went, the older earthbound man would become, while the space traveler would barely age. With the advent of space travel, this theory has been proven, albeit on a minute scale. But then there is the matter of Moses, whose physical body was dust by now. If this was indeed the spirit of Moses, this bizarre reunion would constitute further proof of the interconnectedness between the physical and spiritual planes of existence.

While in the shadow of this "shining cloud," Jesus' face shone or glowed, as did His clothing. This is reminiscent of Moses when he came down from the mountain with the tablets on which were inscribed the Ten Commandments. (Exodus 34: 29.) Moses' face was shining and his hair had turned white. These symptoms are a consequence of exposure to radioactive material. A UFO was in close proximity in both cases. In both cases, those closest to the object displayed symptoms of exposure to radiation.

When the disciples saw the UFO, they fell face down on the ground. Their next conscious recollection was looking up to find Moses and Elijah no longer there. It would seem that something is missing here. Could this be another example of missing time?

Could something have occurred in the interim that had been erased from the disciples' minds?

So Peter spoke up and said to Jesus, "Lord, how good it is that we are here! If you wish, I will make three tents here, one for you, one for Moses and one for Elijah." (Matthew 17: 4.)

What is meant by a "tent" in this instance? Were they referring to a shelter or a place to sleep? If you will recall, in the discussion of Moses' flight from Egypt, he was given specific instructions for the construction of the Ark of the Covenant and the "tent" or the mercy seat. Erik Von Daniken discovered that, when built to the Bible's specifications, the "tent" acted as a form of two-way communication. Apocryphal scripture indicates that this device was still being employed at the time of Jesus' birth.

When they were accordingly met, they unanimously agreed to seek the Lord, and ask counsel from him on this matter. And when they were all engaged in prayer, the high-priest, according to the usual way, went to consult God. And immediately there was a voice from the ark and the mercy seat, which all present heard, that it must be inquired or sought out by a prophecy of Isaiah to whom the virgin should be given and be betrothed. (Mary 5: 11 - 13.)

Whether the reference to a tent meant a shelter or a form of communication with a higher power, it is obvious that the being or beings that communicated with Moses in his day, were still taking an active interest in mankind's development two thousand years later. As Barry Downing observed in "The Bible and Flying Saucers": "The fact that Moses and Elijah were supposedly present at the Transfiguration obviously points to the unity between the Old and New Testaments, as does the presence of the UFO."

If the aerial anomalies witnessed by Moses, Ezekiel, Elijah, and many others in the Old Testament, were indeed metallic crafts manned by physical beings, compared to similar objects witnessed at the birth and throughout the life of Jesus, the assembly at the Transfiguration is strong evidence that the same race of beings was involved.

The "angels" reported in Jesus' time were presumably the same in physical appearance as in the Old Testament. Nothing remarkable was ever mentioned as to their physical appearance, outside of the fact that they wore white robes and descended from a brilliant cloud. Therefore it must be assumed that they looked like any other man. Witnesses knew that earthbound man did not spawn these angels, nor did they have the wherefore-all to create these aerial marvels. Therefore, if the race of man and angel were the same, it must have been the other way around.

Many seemingly miraculous events occurred while Jesus walked the earth. Inexplicable aerial phenomena also surrounded His sojourn through this material plane. Yet, His message to mankind was not of UFOs, outer space or little bugeyed creatures, but that of benevolence, truth, spiritual growth and love. *"The greatest of these is love."* All of these spiritual lessons were taught under the auspices of a spiritual God - not a physical one.

Jesus answered, "You belong to this world here below, but I come from above. You are from this world, but I am not from this world." (John 8: 23) To what world was He referring? A spiritual world, another planet, or both?

"And other sheep I have which are not in this fold. Them also I must bring, and they shall hear my voice and they shall become one flock with one shepherd." (John 10: 16) Where were these "sheep" that Jesus speaks of? To what "fold" did he refer? Other countries on this Earth, other planets in this universe, other dimensions outside of man's range of perception, or all of the above? Surely, if God is the God of the universe, He is all-encompassing.

Chapter 15

So Joseph took it, (Jesus' body) wrapped it in a new linen sheet and placed it in his own tomb, which he had just recently dug out of solid rock. Then he rolled a large stone across the entrance to the tomb and went away. (Matthew 27: 59, 60.)
But Peter got up and ran to the tomb, he bent down and saw the grave cloths but nothing else. Then he went back home amazed at what had happened. (Luke 24:12)

There is no physical evidence more compelling, controversial, mysterious or enduring, that authenticates Jesus' life, death and resurrection, than the Holy Shroud of Turin. (Fig. 8) Few people today are unfamiliar with the fourteen-foot-long piece of linen that, the faithful insist, had wrapped the body of Jesus Christ after his crucifixion and was left behind after his resurrection. The Shroud is kept in a hermetically sealed casket of aluminum and glass, behind gates above the altar in St. John the Baptist Cathedral in Turin, Italy.

After Jesus' tomb was found devoid of a body, the burial Shroud was taken and kept as a Holy Icon. Darkened smudge marks on the cloth seemed to form the faint image of the body that had been wrapped within its fold. Apparent blood stains of the victim are clearly visible on its surface. For almost nineteen hundred years, these smudge marks and blood stains were all that could be seen with the naked eye. Thus, the Shroud was considered to be nothing more than a religious artifact and of little consequence to the scientific community. Then in 1898 the first photograph of the cloth was taken. As the photographer was developing the print, he pulled the negative out of the chemicals to discover a highly detailed image of a man's face. He realized that the image on the Shroud *was* a negative, so the unfinished print that he held in his hand - that should have been a negative - was a positive image. Further photographs revealed the entire torso, frontal and dorsal, extending practically the full length of the cloth. The news of this incredible find brought scientists from around the globe to Turin for the purpose of detailed examination. Of course the church refused to have the Icon picked apart in the interest of science. The Shroud was a matter of faith and the faithful required no scientific confirmation to convince them of its authenticity.

Then, in 1969, an eleven-member team (The Turin Commission) was appointed to establish a criterion for scientific testing and offer advice as to the preservation of the relic. In 1973, Cardinal Pellegrino assembled a panel of experts to examine the cloth. Professor Gilbert Raes was allowed to cut small samples of thread from the cloth. Swiss criminologist Max Frei took twelve samples of surface dust with the use of adhesive tape.

Then in 1978 a small group of scientists, armed with the latest in sleuthing technology, was permitted to subject the cloth to a battery of tests under the watchful eye of its curator. The group had dubbed themselves, STURP (Shroud of Turin Research Project). They wasted no time in setting to the task of attempting to determine the method used to form the image on the Shroud.

Skeptics had suggested that it was nothing more than a painting. The first thing STURP looked for were the brush strokes. There were none to be found. No charcoal, paint or pigmentations of any kind were evidenced on the cloth. That which was assumed to be blood stains were found to have penetrated the fibers of the fabric. Reason dictated that if blood soaked through the fabric, so must have any coloring agent used to render the drawing of the image. To this end they projected a strong light from the back of the cloth. The blood stains were clearly visible but the image was not. This, of course, ruled out the use of any known chemical or coloring agent to render a painting.

Under microscopic observation, they found that while one fiber was discolored, the fiber adjacent to it was not. If the Shroud were man-made, each fiber would have to be colored separately and assembled like a giant tapestry. However, each fiber is one-tenth the diameter of a human hair and, in some areas, the discoloration that forms the image only penetrates the fiber to one-five-hundredth of an inch.

The possibility of the image being a photograph, had already been ruled out. In 1976 the positive photograph of the face on the Shroud was subjected to tests by Dr. John Jackson and Bill

Mottern at Sandia Laboratories in the United States. They employed the use of the VP8 image analyzer, which was used by NASA to interpret images from space. On the screen of the VP8, a two-dimensional photograph of a man's face will appear distorted beyond recognition. The photograph of the face of the man in the Shroud did not. In fact, it formed a perfect relief of a human form, indicating that, however the image was formed, it was done so while being draped over a three-dimensional object - almost surely that of a man.

In 1988, a consortium of three research laboratories received permission to cut another small piece of fabric from the Shroud for the purpose of carbon dating. The result of the carbon-dating test proved devastating to both the scientists and the Christian community. Even though the fabric was determined to be that of a first-century weave, the carbon-14 test indicated that the Shroud dated back to between 1260 and 1390 A.D. The conclusion was drawn, even though the method of rendering the image remained unknown, that the Shroud of Turin was nothing more than a clever medieval forgery.

This setback did not dissuade some of the members of STURP from persevering in their investigations. Too many other clues, suggesting the Shroud's authenticity, had been discovered that could not be so readily dismissed.

The alleged history of the Shroud states that King Abgar of Edessa, north of Jerusalem, had sent for Jesus, having heard of his ability to heal, to cure him of leprosy. By the time word had reached Jerusalem, however, Jesus had been crucified. The Shroud was sent in His stead. The burial cloth had been folded eight times, leaving a rectangle with the image of Jesus' face in the center. King Abgar held the cloth and was miraculously cured.

In 944 the Shroud was moved to Constantinople where it was kept in a church and often put on public display. In 1204, French Crusaders sacked Constantinople and spirited the Shroud off to Europe.

The general consensus of the scientists involved in the study is that the Shroud was in existence in 1350. The carbon-14 dating, as well as church documentation, confirmed this to be a fact. But if this were the date of its origin, it would never have seen daylight in any other location in the world. Further investigations proved this *not* to be the case.

Some researchers today believe that the images of twenty-eight different flower petals can be seen on the Shroud. They were probably placed with the body to honor the dead, such as in today's tradition. All of these flowers were found to be indigenous to the Middle or Near East. With the use of the adhesive tape, microscopic pollen samples were removed from the cloth and examined. Pollen floats, unseen, through the air and will contaminate any surface through mere exposure. It can exist without losing its properties for thousands of years. Out of fifty-eight different pollen specimens found on the cloth, twenty-eight of them exist only in the Middle East. All of the flower impressions and pollen samples found, that could have only been from the Near East, bloom in March or April - around the time observed as Jesus' Passion.

One pollen type, identified as "Gundelia Tournefortii," was found in abundance around the area of the head, where many puncture wounds on the forehead and blood stains on the forehead and in the hair were evident. Gundelia Tournefortii is a noxious weed with many thorny spines protruding from its long leaves. Gundelia Tournefortii grows in only one place on the planet - in and around Jerusalem!

And they platted a crown of thorns and put it upon his head, and a reed in his right hand, and they kneeled down before him and mocked him, saying, "Hail, King of the Jews!"
(Matthew 27: 29)

Further microscopic investigations of material on the adhesive tape revealed limestone, whose properties proved to be indigenous to that of limestone found outside of Jerusalem. It was of the same limestone from which caves were hewn out to serve as tombs.

Despite the carbon-14 dating tests, the aforementioned evidence proved that the Shroud had been in or near Jerusalem at the time that the image was formed and had remained in that vicinity for at least some of its existence.

Dr. Robert Bucklin, M.D., J.D., of Las Vegas, Nevada, had been a forensic pathologist for more than fifty years. He had personally conducted more than twenty-five-thousand autopsies in his long career. In 1997 he conducted an "autopsy" on the Shroud of Turin to determine the cause of death of the man portrayed in it. His findings added fuel to the fires of controversy that had been, for so long, raging. Those findings were as follows:

- The victim was an adult male, seventy-one inches in length and weighing about one-hundred and seventy-five pounds.
- The body is anatomically correct and normal.
- The body appears to be in a state of rigor mortis.
- The left leg had been rotated so that the left foot rested on the right before death. This position remained when rigor mortis had set in. A large blood stain is seen on the left foot.
- The victim had long hair which was formed into a pigtail or braid, as seen in the posterior image. The frontal image shows a mustache and beard. The beard is forked in the middle.
- There is a ring of puncture tracks that encircles the scalp. These puncture tracks are evidenced on both the frontal and dorsal views. Blood had issued in a downward flow from these punctures into the hair and onto the forehead.
- There is an abrasion on the tip of the nose. The right cheek is obviously swollen when compared to the left cheek.
- Although the eyes are closed, close examination reveals small, round, foreign objects on the lids of both eyes. (It was the custom in those days to place coins on the eyelids of the departed loved one, so the lids would not open before glimpsing the next world. Jesuit priest, Father Francis Filas, had discovered a faint image on the eyelids of the man in the Shroud. When the image was subjected to isodensity enhancement, it revealed the objects to possess the exact shape and inscription of the Pontius Pilate lepton coin that was first cast in A.D. 29. Although the identity of the object on the left eye was not so easily discernible, by overlapping the image on the right eye over an actual lepton coin, it was conceded that the image of the coin in the Shroud and its model were struck from the same die.)
- A large blood stain is found on the right pectoral area between the fifth and sixth ribs, over an oval-shaped puncture wound about 4.4 x 1.1 cm. Two types of stains

are found in this area, one is obviously blood, the other appears to be water.

- There is no evidence of spattering from the fluids, indicating that the wound was delivered after the man had expired. (When one is crucified, he must continuously push himself up with his feet. Not to do so would cause him to suffocate due to the outstretched position of the arms. This is why the Romans would break the legs of the victim if they wished to hasten death. When the victim dies of suffocation, water fills the lung cavity. The wound corresponded perfectly to the leaf-shaped point of a Roman "lancea" that had been excavated at Herculaneum.) (*But when they came to Jesus and saw that he was dead already, they break not his legs. But one of the soldiers with a spear pierced his side and forthwith came there out blood and water.*) (John 19: 33, 34.)

- (In 1988, Alan Adler, an assistant professor of molecular biology at the University of Pennsylvania, while investigating the Shroud for the Vatican, determined that the blood came from wounds, because such blood had different chemistry than that of blood flowing in veins.) There is a puncture wound on the left wrist that is covered with a large bloodstain. The left hand overlies the right wrist, hiding whatever wound might be on that wrist. The flow of blood from the wrist wound runs in a horizontal direction, indicating that the arms were outstretched upward at about a sixty-five-degree angle to horizontal when blood was flowing before death. Blood trails are found on both right and left forearms from the wrists to the elbows, which are consistent with the aforementioned calculations.

- (Years ago, a French surgeon, experimenting with cadavers, discovered that a person could not be nailed through the palms of the hands during a crucifixion, as artist's interpretations have always shown and the general populous has grown to accept. The weight of the body would tear through the flesh and let it down. The nail must be driven between the wrist bones to afford adequate support.)

- Only four fingers of both hands are visible, suggesting to the pathologist that, when the wrists were pierced, damage was done to the median nerve, causing the thumbs to turn inward toward the palm, and that position was retained by rigor mortis.

- On the posterior view, the right foot is clearly seen. The same type of puncture wound is observed in the middle of the right foot, suggesting that the same object had penetrated through both feet after the left foot was placed over the right.

- There is a series of blunt-force injuries that are clearly visible on the posterior view, from the shoulders to the small of the back and buttocks and the backs of the calves. Small dumbbell-shaped imprints cover these areas in mass. Blood has issued vertically downward from these wounds, indicating that the man was in an upright position when the blows were delivered, and that his assailant stood behind him. (A Roman instrument of torture called a "flagrum" was secured for the purpose of comparing it to the marks on the back of the man in the Shroud. The flagrum is a short whip with two metal dumbbells at the end of each thong. When the dumbbells were held up to the round impressions on the Shroud, each set of marks matched perfectly in both size and spacing.)

- Abrasions on both right and left shoulder blades were found that are consistent with a heavy object - like a beam - creating a rubbing effect on the skin's surface.

- Dr. Bucklin concluded that the man in the Shroud had suffered numerous injuries by torture and, in light of the placement of blood stains and direction of its flow, he had undergone crucifixion and ultimately died of postural asphyxia. Historically, there is only one person whose death meets with all of the criteria discovered in Dr. Bucklin's examination - Jesus Christ of Nazareth.

What some thought to be red paint on the Shroud, was analyzed and found to indeed be human blood of type AB. What percentage of the world's population shared this blood type when the image was formed is unknown. However, today, only 5 percent of the world's population is known to possess type AB blood. (It must also be pointed out that, according to some experts, most blood more than 120 years old, types to AB.) When the technique of DNA analysis was perfected, Shroud blood samples were once again examined. It has been determined that, not only are all blood specimens throughout the Shroud from the same human being, but that the human being in question was a male of Middle Eastern persuasion.

William Meacham, an archaeologist who uses carbon dating regularly in his work, concludes his findings: "The image was found to be anatomically flawless down to minor details. The characteristic features of rigor mortis, wounds, and blood flows provided conclusive evidence to the anatomists that the image was formed by direct or indirect contact with a corpse, not painted onto the cloth or scorched thereon by a hot statue. On this point all medical opinion since the time of Delage has been unanimous."

Yet there are those scientists that must provide the world with an answer to every scientific mystery, that fits within the confines of accepted world-view, regardless of how loosely their conclusions fit the evidence. If they are unable to supply such an answer, they will assign one - to wit, in the case of the Shroud, a clever Medieval painting.

But what would such a clever fraud entail? For the Shroud to be that of "artistic fraud," someone in thirteenth-century Europe would have to have used a coloring agent unknown to mankind to this day. He would have had to reconstruct a linen cloth of a first-century weave. Then secure at least twenty-eight flora specimens from Jerusalem, along the Dead Sea, up through Constantinople and into Europe. He must, then, meticulously reproduce these flowers on the cloth and spread their pollen evenly over it. He must secure the Roman lancea and flagrum to be used as models for the proper size and spacing of the wounds. This done, he would have had to create an anatomically correct image of a man who bore the marks of scourging and crucifixion, using human blood with its flow in the proper direction from each wound, indicating the position in which he was when the wound was administered. Thus, not only corresponding to exact detail as given in scripture, but to details widely unknown at that time (such as the necessity of driving the nail through the wrist instead of the palm). The coup de grace of this alleged forgery is that he would have had to paint the whole image, front and back, in *negative*, in the hopes that, one day, mankind would invent photography to expose the *positive* image in its entirety. Such a feat would be more miraculous than the resurrection itself!

In this author's opinion, those who believe that highly trained and well-seasoned forensic pathologists from America and Europe are unable to tell the difference between an actual corpse and a painting, should stand in line with those who believe that highly trained and well-seasoned, high-ranking officers in the US Air Force are unable to tell the difference between a weather balloon and a flying disk.

Yet another Holy Icon exists that tends to muddy the scientific waters for the skeptic and help validate the position of the believer. That is the Sudarium, or face cloth, reportedly found in Jesus' tomb alongside the Shroud.

Behind him came Simon Peter, and he went straight into the tomb. He saw the linen cloths lying there and the cloth which had been around Jesus' head. It was not lying with the linen cloths but was rolled up by itself. (John 20: 6, 7.)

The American Standard Version refers to it as a "napkin," indicating the difference in size from that of the Shroud. It is also referred to as the "second cloth."

The Sudarium also bears blood stains and the faint negative image of the man in the Shroud, albeit not as distinct. It had been moved from Jerusalem, ahead of an advancing Persian Army, along the African coast to Toledo, Spain. In 711 A.D., during the Moorish invasion of Spain, it was smuggled out and moved northward where it was hidden in a cave for safe keeping. The Sudarium now makes its home in The Cathedral of Saint John in Oviedo, Spain.

When the image of the Sudarium is overlaid on that of the Shroud of Turin, the position of the head, its facial features and the blood stains, correlate precisely. The blood on the Sudarium was also examined and found to be of type AB. In light of these findings, logic would dictate that, despite their geographical variance, the images on the Sudarium and the Shroud of Turin were produced at the same time, while draped over the same corpse.

Historical records undeniably prove that the Sudarium has been in Spain since the seventh century. This fact alone would undercut the carbon-dating results of the Shroud by six-hundred years. Because of this fact, the accuracy of carbon-14 dating analysis is brought into question. However, the accuracy of carbon-dating can well be relied upon if all factors are taken into consideration. One factor that was unknown at the time of the 1988 carbon-dating test was later discovered by Dr. Leoncio Garza-Valdes. While testing Mayan artifacts, he found that, over time, bacteria, from exposure to the elements, produces an organic or "bioplastic coating" on textiles. This bioplastic coating can distort the results of the carbon-14 process. Any such contaminated object, subjected to the carbon-dating process, is actually significantly older than test results indicate.

In 1996, the Shroud was reexamined and found to possess a significant amount of this contamination. Due to the fact that investigators were unaware of the bioplastic coating problem during the original test, the cleaning process that was employed was insufficient in eliminating it from the Shroud's surface. As of this writing, scientists are still attempting to discover a method for separating the coating from the Shroud without damaging its fibers or adversely affecting the test results. Whether authorities will permit another carbon-dating test, if and when a safe process is found, remains to be seen.

The closest explanation that STURP experts can arrive at is that the image was the result of a chemical change known as "dehydrated oxidation." Exactly what caused that chemical change is still a matter of speculation. When it comes down to the bottom line, the scientific experts can tell us what it is not - they cannot tell us what it is.

There is one more curious and unprecedented factor about the Shroud that I have purposely saved until last. In some areas of the body where the skin is most thin, the bones of the man in the shroud are clearly visible. These areas are most notably the hands and wrists. However, the shinbone and teeth (complete with roots) are seen. It's as if an overlay of the flesh had been placed over the bones in these areas. Pathologists and anatomists agree that: (1) the bones are anatomically perfect and not the result of an artist's rendering and (2) this X-ray effect could only have been accomplished with the introduction of one element - radiation!

If radiation was the factor involved in producing the X-ray effect, it could well be the method by which the image itself was formed. One theory as to how the image was produced, is that a strong light had left a shadow on the cloth of the man who had lain within it. When the atom bomb was detonated at Hiroshima, there were people standing in front of a wall that were vaporized by the blast. The brilliant flash of light had bleached out the wall, leaving only the indelible shadows of those that had stood between it and the source of the light.

But even if a corpse could generate that kind of power, there is still the question of the radiation. There were no devices that required nor produced radiation two thousand years ago. Even if the body of Jesus did produce the light and radiation, it would not account for the image of the coins on the eyelids. If the light was generated outward from within the Shroud, the shape of the coins would be discernable but not the inscription on their face. The light, whose properties included radiation, must have been external.

STURP members have concluded that, if radiation was involved in producing the image, it would have so altered the chemical makeup of the cloth that further carbon-dating tests would prove pointless.

And in the night in which the Lord's day was drawing on, as the soldiers kept guard two by two in a watch, there was a great voice in the heaven, and they saw the heavens open, and two men descend from thence with great light and approach the tomb. And that stone which was put at the door rolled of itself and made way in part, and the tomb was opened, and both the young men entered in. (The Apocrypha. The Gospel According to Peter. Verse 9)

And while they yet thought thereon, the heavens again are seen to open, and a certain man to descend and enter into the sepulcher. (The Apocrypha. The Gospel According to Peter. Verse 11.)

Here again is the familiar phrase, "the heavens/sky opened." Again, beings that are recognizable as men (sans wings) descend from the opening in a "great light." The witnesses heard a "great voice," but it is not clear as to whether the voice had spoken in comprehensible words, since none were mentioned, or if there was merely a noise such as was heard by Ezekiel (a sound like the *roar of the sea, like the noise of a huge army, like the voice of Almighty God*). The aforementioned passages also attest to the fact that neither a man nor an angel had rolled the stone away from the mouth of the cave. It clearly states that the stone *"rolled of itself."*

Betty Andreasson Luca, in "The Watchers," recalled under hypnosis, while aboard a craft during one of her abduction experiences, seeing a light that was so bright that she could see right through her hand. It would seem that this is the kind of intensity necessary to create the shadow of Jesus on the Shroud.

When the UFO shone its beam down on the tomb, the anti gravitational properties within it were responsible for removing the stone with great ease. The instant the stone had been removed, the brilliant beam shone into the cave and directly onto the Shroud which enveloped the body of Jesus. The electromagnetic radiation that is a consequence of the craft's propulsion system (and has, all too often, been reported to adversely affect so many close encounter UFO witnesses and abductees) literally permeated Jesus' body, causing the image on both the front and back of the Shroud and producing the X-ray effect. Whatever property the light possessed that reanimated the physical body, most likely had to do with that which causes reverse polarization of the atoms. The same properties that allow abductees and their captors to traverse, unscathed, through walls and windows. The same properties that allow the descent and ascent of the so-called "aliens" of today and the so-called "angels" of the Biblical era.

In John 20: 17, when Mary Magdalene confronts Jesus on the day of his resurrection, he tells her not to touch him as he has not yet ascended to the Father. If reverse polarization accounted for the reanimation of Jesus' body, most likely Mary's hand would have gone right through him, as if she were attempting to touch a hologram. Reverse polarization would also account for Jesus' appearance in the "Upper Room." The doors were reportedly locked, yet Jesus had gained access and stood amongst them. (John 20: 26.) Although Jesus offered Thomas to put his finger in his hand and side, there is no mention of Thomas having taken him up on that offer. The offer to do so alone was enough to convince him of Jesus' identity. (John 20: 27, 28.)

Jesus appeared in five separate locations on five different occasions within the forty-day period between his resurrection and ascension. Nowhere in scripture does it specifically state that anyone had placed their hands upon him.

Jesus finally departed this earthly incarnation outside of Jerusalem after assuring his disciples that he would return: *After saying this, he was taken up to heaven as they watched him, and a cloud hid him from their sight.* (Acts 1: 9.) Then, in the presence of eyewitnesses, Jesus was levitated up into that brilliant cloud that had come to be synonymous with "the Glory of God."

Conclusion

In September of 1981, an article by Ulrich Dopatka appeared in a bimonthly publication known as "Ancient Skies," published by the Ancient Astronaut Society. The article recounted several documented incidents that are strikingly similar to ancient myth and Biblical scripture. In it he observes that, by the beginning of the twentieth century, few places on Earth were untouched by modern technology. Exceptions to this included remote areas in the South American jungles, the African Kalahari, the jungles of New Guinea, and the Pacific Island of Melanesia and Micronesia.

The natives of Tanna, on the Island of Melanesia, have a unique religion. They worship a god whose name is "John Frum." They have tattooed their skin with a symbol, for which even they do not understand the meaning of - "USA." It is said that, a long time ago, the king of a far away land called "America" came to this remote island and, for a time, lived among them. Unlike the Melanesians, he was tall and of a fair complexion. He gave the natives many strange artifacts as a goodwill offering. These included coins and paper money, a helmet and a photograph of a man. (Whether the man was Frum or someone else is unknown.) Although he spoke a strange language, Frum learned to communicate and shared with them the secrets of nature. He explained to them about lightning, sound, wind and the constellations of the heavens. In an expedition to Tanna in the 1970's, by westerners, they found the entire nation anxiously awaiting their god, John Frum, to return to them from the kingdom of America.

A small band of Spanish conquistadors conquered nations with millions of people, because the natives thought that they (the Spaniards) were their returning gods. Another small band of men, headed by Hernando Cortez, conquered the Aztec empire because the natives believed him to be their god Quetzalcoatl. Cortez was tall, bearded and of a fair complexion, as was the description of the visiting god that had been handed down by their ancestors.

Quetzalcoatl had promised to return from across the waters to the East, as did Cortez.

When Captain James Cook arrived on the island of Tahiti in the South Pacific, the natives believed him to be their god "Rongo," who had visited them long before. He had arrived and departed in a "sky ship."

A helicopter had flown a group of ethnologists in to visit the Tasaday people in the Philippines. The natives immediately fell to their knees and worshiped the "big bird." They had seen this spectacular vision before and knew that it, and the strange-looking people that it bore, were responsible for bringing them presents from the gods.

However, not all such heavenly vehicles were revered as gods. When the Papuas of New Guinea first witnessed a landing seaplane, they referred to it as, "the devil who came down from the sky."

During his expedition to New Guinea in 1920, Frank Hurley found that the natives had constructed wooden models of his seaplane and distributed them to all the households. Natives from the Eastern highlands of New Guinea erected bamboo "radio stations" to represent the Persian Oil Company's transmitter, which was responsible for bringing them free cargo. What is most interesting, is that they had built airports and landing strips in the jungle in the hope that the gods would bring them even more presents. Shortly after World War II, the natives on a small New Guinean island constructed a similar airport and adorned it with bamboo airplanes to await the return of the gods that had brought them many wonderful and mysterious gifts. Could this have been the purpose of the ancient Nazca lines in Peru? If you will recall, some of the Nazca lines appear to be laid out for the same purpose.

These are but a few examples of an advanced civilization's intrusion on a primitive one. The technology that was witnessed by the natives was nothing short of miraculous to them. The human beings that operated these vehicles were of a fairer complexion, different facial features and bone structure than their own, and were clad in totally unfamiliar attire. The natives thought that they and their little island paradise were all that existed under a canopy of celestial marvels. They were the only living intelligent beings in the world! They probably even thought that the world on which they dwelled was perfectly flat. As far as the inhabitants of these islands were concerned, what else could these events represent if not visitations from the gods?

This sentiment has been echoed by mankind, from all corners of the Earth, since the dawn of his introduction to physical existence. His arrogance in the belief that he is the only intelligent life in the universe, other than Almighty God, has disallowed him from accepting any possibility of the existence of intelligent, extraterrestrial life.

Then, enters on the scene, visitors from the galactic neighborhood. Their "flying chariots of fire" are spectacular and their awe-inspiring powers are mind-boggling. The beings that float down from them, heralding spiritual messages and dictating moral standards for Earth's inhabitants, could only be the angels of God. One by one, their visits, words and deeds are witnessed and recorded for posterity. Some of which are recorded on stone walls - some on parchment. Some find their way to word-of-mouth legends. Only those records deemed worthy by a select few are reprinted, translated and set to book form - "The Book" - and a religion is born.

Some abductees would be quick to differ with the idea that these visitors are benevolent. When one considers the manner in which they are rudely snatched from their beds, cars and other locations, and subjected to physically and emotionally painful examinations and experimentations, by odd-looking and seemingly indifferent beings, their reasoning can hardly be argued with. Their need to keep the alien reality and their chosen religious beliefs as two very diverse entities, is completely understandable. Their faith is the only source of comfort they have to fall back on in an otherwise surreal and frightening existence. How devastating it would be to realize that the source of their fears and that of their faith is all part and parcel of the same phenomenon.

But consider Christopher Columbus and his men arriving in "the new world." What must the Native Americans have thought when they witnessed these huge "canoes" with massive sheets to catch the wind? Aboard were fair skinned men with hair on their faces, clad in strange looking costumes. They sported sticks of fire that could take a life from some distance. Their language was incomprehensible and their customs were more than strange. A vision such as that must have been next to impossible to fathom. Yet, there they were!

The first wave of white men wanted only to share the land and embark upon a new beginning. For this purpose, the Native Americans welcomed them. Then came the next wave, whose agendas were varied and, for most, unscrupulous. Some would pillage the land and its people, pushing its rightful owners westward and taking many of their lives in the process. The diverse reasons for making the perilous journey are too numerous to recount here. However, some came as missionaries for the purpose of enlightening the natives as to spiritual matters that had been passed down to them from the missionaries that had inspired the scriptures.

Were some or all of the miraculous visions, witnessed by those who committed their experiences to parchment, the same unexplainable aerial phenomena being witnessed by modern man? The parallels between Biblical and modern-day descriptions of the experiences, presented in this book, lend credence to that possibility.

Even though the spirit of Jesus was, at best, the Son of the living "Spiritual God," and, at least, one of the most highly advanced souls in God's universe, it was necessary for that soul to incarnate into a physical body in which to intermingle and directly communicate with other souls who were trapped in physical bodies. Mankind was regarding the missionaries of God as God Himself. It was imperative that a representative of the spiritual realm walk among men as one of them, so that the line of demarcation could be drawn. That physical body could *not* have been the product of a physical mother and a spiritual father. The genetic engineering abilities that have been demonstrated by our alien visitors leave little doubt that those abilities were known and practiced by the alien visitors of the Biblical era. Even so, how would it have been possible to introduce the proper spiritual entity to the designated body without a direct connection between the physical beings, conducting the artificial insemination of Mary, and the spiritual realm?

Betty Andreason Luca, previously mentioned, underwent an out-of-body experience at the hands of her alien abductors. She was soon to learn why this method was necessary, as opposed to *physical* abduction. Her spiritual entity was taken to what the greys referred to as, "the great door." Beyond the doorway was a brilliant light. A man with long white hair, dressed in a white robe, whom she equated to an angel, was clearly visible on the other side. As with near-death experiencers, she found it impossible to describe, in earthly terms, the beauty, serenity, peace and love, with which she was enveloped, merely by the sight of this divine illumination. Her hosts referred to it as "the glory of the One." Betty was made to understand that this was for everyone and that everyone would, one day, experience it. They assured her that everyone and everything are a part of "the One." ("The Watchers." Page 144)

Was Betty's "great door" the same door referred to by my cousin Steve's father in chapter seven? ("I have to go now. Steve is waiting for me at *the door*.") Was it the same door that I had seen during my own OBE, when I was told, "we are not ready for you yet."? Was this great light, which exudes peace and unconditional love, the same as has been reported by NDE patients around the world, from age three to ninety-three? Was it the light that, as the beings promised, everyone will witness on the day of their physical demise? Was the being of light that Betty witnessed beyond the door, one of those messengers that, on occasion, has visited mankind in the past to herald the good news of an eternal hereafter? Are the mediators, between our physical realm and the spiritual realm, now and always have been, missionaries from a neighboring star or parallel dimension, who have come to spread the gospel to this tiny island, Earth? Has this always been the brunt of the messages that the visitors have been bringing since the advent of humankind? And what is most important, was Jesus Christ of Nazareth the culmination of a terrestrial woman, an extraterrestrial man and the spirit of the Son of the one true Creator of all things?

After a lifetime of confusing and disturbing abduction experiences, these questions were finally answered for Betty Luca. She was alone in her home one afternoon, when she felt the uncontrollable urge to walk out to the woods behind the house. There she was greeted by one of the greys that had, for years, been a great source of upheaval in her life. By now she was not afraid of them - only concerned as to what might follow. This time, however, he was not there to take her away. He was there to deliver a message and to ease her mind as to their objective and her role in it.

On page 334 of "The Watchers," Betty recounts the experience while under hypnosis. The following are her words from the taped transcript:

"He has been sent and I am not to fear. The Lord is with me

and I am not to be afraid. They are pleased because I have accepted Christianity on my own. I am to go through many things and that love will show me the answers because I have given my heart over to love the *Son*. Many things shall be revealed to me. Things that I have not seen - ears have not heard. I shall suffer many things but will overcome them through the *Son*. I have been watched since my beginning. I shall grow naturally and my faith in the Light will bring many others to the Light and salvation because many will understand and see. The negative voices don't like it. They are against man. Bad angels that wanted to devour man - hurt man - destroy man, because they are jealous of the love that is upon man. Telling me strange things. I don't know what they're about. That for every place there is an existence. That every thing has been formed to unite. He says, Jesus is with me. That I will understand as time goes by. For me not to be anxious. They want me to grow and live naturally. That I am blessed and that I will forget and I am now to go back to my house and I will not remember. He says, 'Peace be with you, as it is.'"

This visit and clarification by her abductors helped to demonstrate to Betty the benevolent purpose of the race of beings that she had been confronted with all of her life.

Some people refer to themselves as "abductees" and others wish to be referred to as "experiencers." The differences being that, the former group of people view their abductions as highly intrusive and frightening. They feel exploited and abused by a race of beings that regard them as little more than lab rats, to be studied and experimented with. They don't understand the aliens' objectives or their own involvement in it. Furthermore, they sense that their captors are completely indifferent to their plight. Therefore, they are highly suspicious of the aliens' intent and doubt that any objective that they may have, could be anything other than sinister.

The latter, however, view the aliens' purpose as benevolent. They feel that, because of their experiences, they are involved in the quest of a "higher purpose." They have been told by the beings that they have been around since the dawn of mankind. They were responsible for the seeding of our race upon the Earth and continue to act as custodians for our world. Both ancient legend and Holy Scripture, as mentioned in previous chapters, lend strong circumstantial evidence to support their claim. *They* are the "watchers."

In the early fifteen-hundreds, men from all walks of life came to the American Colonies with both good and evil agendas. So it has been in the case of our *galactic* voyagers. In John 5: 45, Jesus said of God, *"For He makes His Sun to shine on bad and good people alike and gives rain to those who do good and to those who do evil."* Therefore, it is not surprising to hear two very diverse sentiments concerning the same experience. It is simply a matter of which side of the "abduction coin" they find themselves on.

If the very human-looking aliens were indeed responsible for the advent of the human race, then to refer to them as "god," would be grammatically correct (in the sense of the creator, the author, founder etc.) However, such a reference would apply only to the physical. The spiritual God is, and always has been the creator of all souls. Not only ours, but those of the visitors and any other physical or spiritual life forms that may exist in this vast cosmos. The visitors are not only more advanced technologically, mentally and physically, but also spiritually. They have realized that, even though mankind, for the most part, has accepted their message pertaining to the spiritual realm and the continued existence of the soul, they also realize that we have confused their presence with that of the spiritual God. We have assumed that spiritual and physical "miracles" are all part and parcel of the same Godly phenomena, and have built our varied religions to suit.

It was for this reason that they arranged for one of their own to walk among us, in the person of the man we call Jesus Christ of Nazareth. His mission was to help us to differentiate between the physical messengers from the sky and the spiritual plane that exists, not in any *one* location in the cosmos, but "within our midst." Jesus' incarnation proved to be the perfect marriage of a terrestrial and extraterrestrial physical body, animated by the soul of the Son of the one, true, spiritual God.

So many seemingly miraculous events were witnessed and recorded from the time of Jesus' conception to his ascension. So many seemingly miraculous aerial phenomena surrounded the major events in his life. The western orthodox church will tell us that the "age of miracles" is over. Perhaps this is the reason that we do not view the UFO/abduction phenomenon as a miracle, but a totally separate entity from that of faith. Yet, when the UFO/abduction phenomenon is overlaid on similar events reported in the Holy Bible, Apocrypha and other related texts, their appearance and texture seem to meld as one. Perhaps, then, there is no such thing as miracles. The word, by it's very definition, suggests an event that occurs outside of the laws of nature. I contend that *nothing* can occur that is outside the laws of nature - simply that which is outside of our understanding of natural law. If this is the case, then perhaps what we have perceived as miracles are merely glimpses of a larger reality, the scope of which, we are only now beginning to comprehend.

Yet, in spite of all of the correlations between Biblical text and UFO documentation, it is still difficult to incorporate the two subjects as one - especially in the light of orthodox doctrine that has saturated our minds throughout our lives. Making this connection was one of the most grueling tasks that I have had to undergo in my life. Though I do not claim to be the most devout Christian in the world, I too have grown up in a church-oriented atmosphere and have come to accept Biblical text as fact. After years of investigation and a lot of soul-searching, the connection, outlined in this book, has become my ultimate and inescapable conclusion. What would it take, then, for the most devout Christian to make that same connection? One must first acknowledge the fact that all things in God's universe are, in some way, connected.

My mother, a devout Orthodox Christian all of her life, made that connection years ago. She never acknowledged it - she never even realized it - and yet, the connection was made.

"It's the second coming!" she declared, as our family stood on our front lawn, one silent summer's night, and gazed in awe upon technology . . . millennia beyond our time.

Author's Note.

For the reader who is new to the studies of the UFO/abduction phenomenon and metaphysics, and would like to learn more about the subject, I invite you to read some or all of the books listed in the Bibliography. I caution you, however, each book has its own Bibliography that could snowball into a learning frenzy. The subject is addictive and the documented evidence is provocative and eye-opening.

Don't allow this one book to sway your opinion in one direction. Study as much as possible on these matters and draw your own conclusions.

(Figure 1)

Egyptian hieroglyph of ancient light bulb. Discovered in southern Egypt in the Temple of Dendera.

(Figure 2)

Eric Von Daniken reproduced the ancient light bulb, according to the instructions found in the temple. It successfully illuminated.

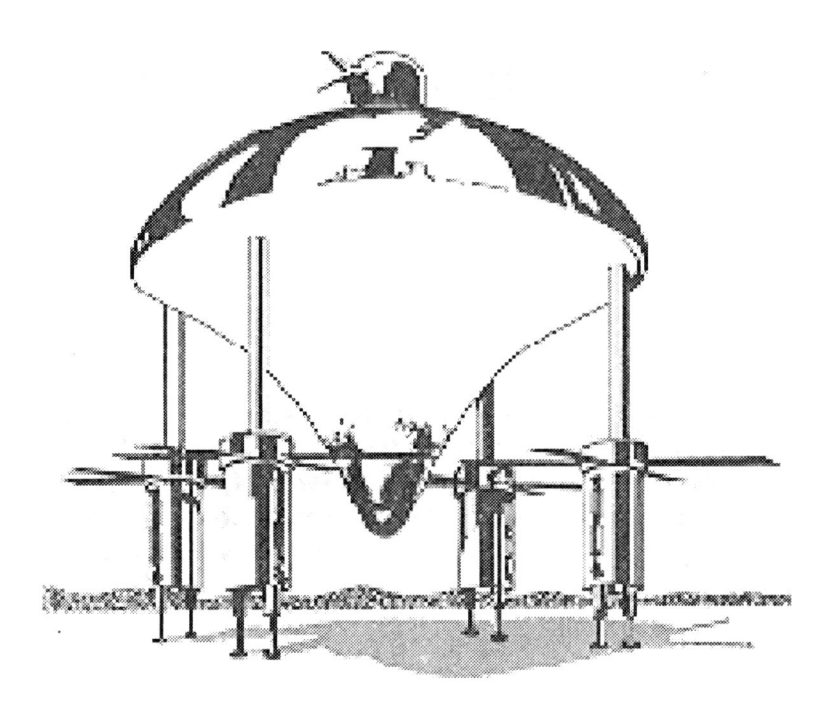

(Figure 3)

This is a drawing of Josef F. Blumrich's design of the landing craft witnessed by Ezekiel. The crew's compartment sits above a nuclear reactor. The four cylindrical landing supports, with mechanical arms hanging down at their sides, could easily be interpreted as "living beings" to someone in fifth century BC. The "wings" of the "living beings" are helicopter blades that whirl to lift the craft, and fold down over their bodies when at rest.

(Figure 4)

Blumrich's concept of the "wheel within a wheel" affording the craft universal movement.

(Figure 5)

An artist's rendition of the Eagle landing on the surface of the moon. Compare this vehicle with the verbal description of Ezekiel's vision.

(Figure 6)

God in His chariot of fire from a mural in Desani Monastery in Yugoslavia.

(Figure 7)

A Nativity scene Painted in the Renaissance period, found in Palazzo Vecchio in Florence. It has been attributed to the 15th Century school of Filippo Lippi. Note the object in the sky over Mary's left shoulder and the man and dog in the background looking up at it. (Blowup)

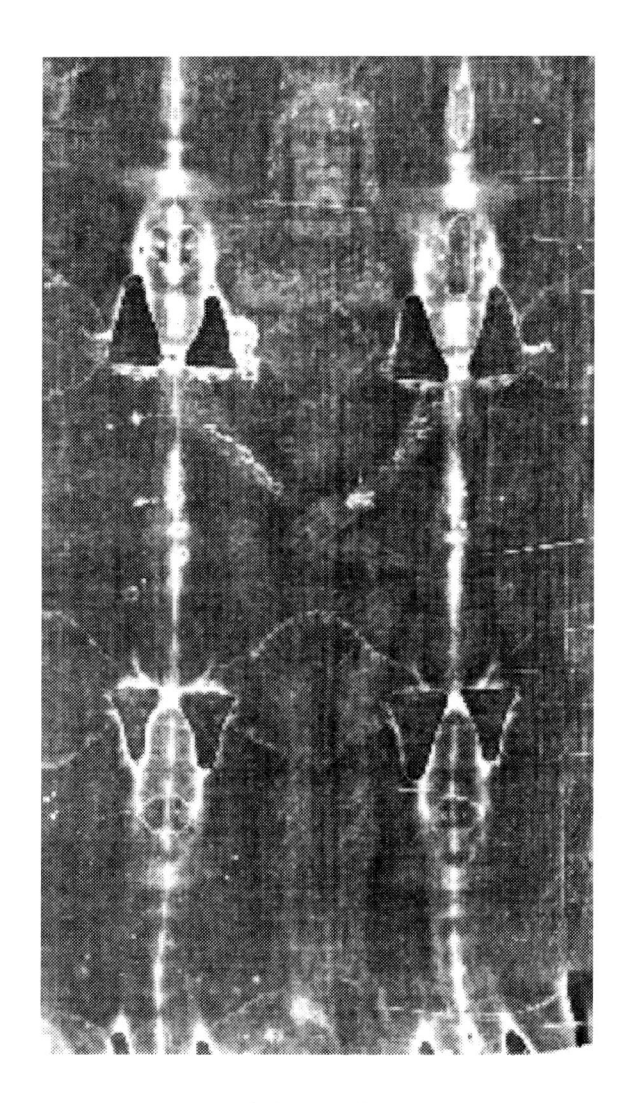

(Figure 8)

The Shroud of Turin. Believed to be the cloth that wrapped the body of Jesus Christ. This is the negative image of the shroud. The image on the cloth itself is a negative. Thus, the negative on the film (before processing) comes out as a positive image.

Bibliography

Daniken, Erik Von, Chariots of the Gods? New York, Putnam's, 1970.

Blumrich, Josef F. The Spaceships of Ezekial. New York, Bantam Books, 1974.

Fuller, John G. The Interrupted Journey. New York, Dell Publishing Co. 1967.

Good News Bible. Today's English Version - Second edition. New York, The American Bible Society, 1992.

The Holy Bible. American Standard Version. New York, Thomas Nelson & Sons, 1901.

Davenport, Marc. Visitors From Time. The Secret of the UFOs. Murfreesboro, TN. Greenleaf Publications. 1994.

Good, Timothy. Above Top Secret: The Worldwide UFO Cover-up. New York, Morrow, 1988.

Downing, Barry. The Bible and Flying Saucers. New York, Marlowe & Company, 1968.

Bill Guggenheim & Judy Guggenheim. Hello From Heaven! New York, Bantam Books, 1995.

Moody, Raymond A. Jr., M.D. Life After Life. Covington, Georgia, Mockingbird Books. 1975.

Muldoon, Sylvan & Carrington, Hereward. The Projection of The Astral Body. York Beach, ME. Samuel Weiser, Inc., 1973.

Bernstein, Morey. The Search for Bridey Murphy. Garden City, New York. Doubleday. 1956.

Backer, William J. The Search for Bridey Murphy With New Material. Garden City, New York. Doubleday. 1965.

Weiss, Brian L. Many Lives, Many Masters. New York. Simon and Schuster. 1988

Stevenson, Ian, M.D. Twenty Cases Suggestive of Reincarnation. (Revised. 2nd. edition) University Press of Virginia. 1974.

Furst, Jeffrey. Edgar Cayce's Story of Jesus. New York. Coward, McCann and Geoghegan, Inc. 1976.

Walton, Travis. Fire in The Sky; The Walton Experience. New York. Marlow & Co. 1974.

Hopkins, Budd. Witnessed: The True Story of the Brooklyn Bridge UFO Abductions. New York. Pocket Books/Simon & Schuster. 1996.

Hopkins, Bud. Intruders. New York. Random House. 1987.

Fowler, Raymond E. The Watchers: The Secret Design Behind UFO Abduction. New York. Bantam Books. 1990.

The Lost Books of The Bible and The Forgotten Books of Eden. World Bible Publishing, Inc. 1927.

Hopkins, Budd. Intruders. N.Y. Random House. 1987.

Articles and other Sources.

Smith, Malcolm. Are Hybrids Impossible? MUFON, UFO Journal. September 1998. #365. Page 15.

The Shroud of Turin Web site. http://shroud.com/index.htm Barrie M.Schwortz

Robert Bucklin, M.D., J.D. An Autopsy on the Man of the Shroud

Filas, Francis. 1982. The dating of the Shroud of Turin from coins of Pontius Pilate. Youngtown, Ariz.: Cogan Productions. [ADW]

Frei, Max. 1982. Nine years of palynological studies on the Shroud. Shroud Spectrum International 1(3): 3-7.

McNair, Philip. 1978. "The Shroud and history: Fantasy, fake, or fact?" in Face to Face with the Turin Shroud. Edited by Peter Jennings, pp. 21-40. Oxford: Mowbray.

Raes, G. 1976. "Rapprt d'analyse du tissu," in La S. Sindone, pp. 79-84. Turin: Diocesi Torinese.

Friedman, Stanton. UFOs . . . The Real Story. Multimedia CD-ROM for Windows. Unity Publishing. 1996.

Dopatka, Ulrich. (Translated from German by Yvonne Dunnenberger.) Ancient Skies. Volume 8. Number 4. The Ancient Astronaut Society. Highland Park, Illinois. Sept. 1981. Web site: www.aas-ra.org

Mike's UFO Connection web site. http://www.primenet.com/~msebring/index.html

Photograph of the Eagle moon lander compliments of NASA/TRW. Web site: http://ston.jsc.nasa.gov/

Figures 1 and 2 compliments of Giorgio A. Tsoukalos of The Legendary Times. http://www.legendarytimes.com

Figures 3 and 4 compliments of http://earthportals.com/Portal_Ship/ezekiel.html